Planting and Maintaining a Tree Collection

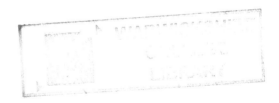

Planting and Maintaining a
Tree Collection

▲▲▲

Simon Toomer

Timber Press
Portland ▲ London

All photographs are by the author unless otherwise noted.
Frontispiece: Birches and wood anemones. Photo by Steve Wooster,
© Forestry Commission.

Published in 2010 by Timber Press, Inc.

The Haseltine Building   2 The Quadrant
133 S.W. Second Avenue, Suite 450   135 Salusbury Road
Portland, Oregon 97204-3527   London NW6 6RJ
www.timberpress.com   www.timberpress.co.uk

Printed in China

Library of Congress Cataloging-in-Publication Data

Toomer, Simon.
   Planting and maintaining a tree collection / Simon Toomer.
       p. cm.
   Includes bibliographical references and index.
   ISBN 978-0-88192-930-0
   1. Trees—Collection and preservation. 2. Arboretums. I. Title.
   QK479.T66 2010
   635.9'77—dc22
                                           2009036881

A catalog record for this book is also available from the British Library.

*This book is dedicated to Westonbirt Arboretum,
home to some of the finest trees in the world and
my continuing source of inspiration.*

Contents

Color plates follow page 96

Acknowledgements

The author would like to thank the following people and organisations for their help and encouragement with the writing of this book:

Anna Mumford
The staff at Westonbirt Arboretum, particularly Hugh Angus, Mark Ballard, Sally Day, Penny Jones, and Ben Oliver
Bedgebury National Pinetum
The Forestry Commission
Paul Wynen, Eastwoodhill Arboretum
Tony Aiello and Paul Meyer, Morris Arboretum
The National Memorial Arboretum
Arnold Arboretum
David Binnian, Bodenham Arboretum
Wolfgang Bopp, Sir Harold Hillier Gardens
Piers Newth, Harcourt Arboretum
Ian Turner, Sheffield Botanical Gardens
Hilary Smith
My family, for their help and patience

1 ▲ Why Grow Trees?
Introduction to Tree Collecting

When it comes to popularity, trees have an almost universal following. For many people, this is explained by their physical presence and beauty. For more studious types, they represent the ultimate expression of plant evolution and thereby endless possibility for study and learning. Trees and shrubs by definition have a framework of woody trunks and branches designed to give them an advantage over their herbaceous plant counterparts when it comes stature and longevity. This means that a tree planted today will not only grow to provide satisfaction for the planter but also flourish and develop for perhaps centuries, giving subsequent guardians ample opportunity for appreciation. (PLATE 1)

Mankind is an acquisitive species with a strong instinct to gather together things that have a practical use or aesthetic beauty, or simply invoke curiosity. Add to this a desire to understand, categorise, and exhibit, and you have the basic characteristics of the collector. Whether it be postage stamps, antique vases, or something with no financial value at all, most of us have, at some time, set out to collect something that interests us and fulfils an urge to track down and acquire. For some, this becomes a lifetime's passion with increasing knowledge leading to more carefully considered aims, objectives, and self-imposed constraints. Others carry on their collecting in a more haphazard way, relying on subjective impulse rather than planned process for direction. In the end, whatever approach is taken, the judgment of success depends on the objectives set, whether they be scientific, artistic, or simply to pleasurably fill a few leisure hours.

Though the collecting of trees may, at first consideration, seem very different from that of inanimate objects, the same principles apply, and those that follow the pursuit are driven by the same motivations. The mortality of trees may be considered a disadvantage over dead objects as collectibles, but this is amply compensated for by their ability to regenerate and change with time. Like museum pieces, trees have attributes worthy of measuring and recording, and investigation beyond their simple physical presence often reveals a fascinating web of scientific and cultural associations. But unlike items in a museum, trees and shrubs are large plants that are grown in gardens. They needn't be arranged in serried ranks according to their taxonomic grouping but in more imaginative or aesthetically pleasing ways to inform, entertain, or just look good. Indeed, many visitors to even well-labelled tree collections take some convincing to regard them as collections at all. Most commonly, trees will be combined with non-woody plants in a variety of garden settings. They may provide the structural element and continuity in the designed landscape as well as providing shade or shelter to smaller or less hardy plants. Where trees and shrubs are grown in more specialised collections, the garden is often referred to as an arboretum or, where conifers are the dominant plants, a pinetum. The definition of these may vary, but it should allow for and reflect the rich variety of possibilities. The following definition does that and also identifies the three most common objectives in a simple way: an arboretum is "a place where an extensive variety of woody plants is cultivated for scientific, educational, and ornamental purposes." Of course "scientific" is a wide description that can include commercial and conservation aims as well as many others.

Many collectors slip into the habit almost by accident. The initial seed of interest may be a chance encounter with a tree in full bloom or at a particular location, but once the connection is made that species or group becomes a favourite to be sought and collected. Some people happily carry on for years, building up a long and impressive list of species without even realising they have become collectors. As far as they are concerned, they are simply filling their gardens with the plants they want to grow. But almost inevitably, somewhere along the line, they will begin to specialise or develop a particular preference for some group or other. Some plants attract more adoration than others for obvious reasons, but even the least glamorous have their passionate advocates, and the concept of inverted snobbery is alive and well in the world of plant collecting. For some collectors, excitement lies not in the gaudy flowers or delicately lobed leaves of popular garden trees but the subtle variation between a number of closely related and rather obscure species that most gardeners wouldn't give border space to. From then on, it's only a short step to carefully recording the plants collected and maybe even swapping with like-minded collectors elsewhere.

Some collections have no definite starting point but develop from an existing arboretum or other tree planting when someone decides to plot and identify them and perhaps write a plan for their maintenance and long-term replanting. These "captured" collections are particularly valuable for institutions like schools where the trees can provide immediate subject matter for study.

A long tradition

The tradition of collecting and growing trees has a long and distinguished history. Depending on where they happen to live in the world, anyone with an interest in their native flora will get to know the range of trees that inhabit their local woods and farmland. For those lucky enough to live in one of nature's more diverse habitats, the list of species may run to many hundreds, if not thousands. For others, the task of learning will be much easier. Inhabitants of the British Isles, for example, have only about thirty-five or so native trees, their land having never regained much of its tree flora lost during the ravages of the last Ice Age and subsequent isolation from mainland Europe. Look today however at the vast number and infinite variety of trees to be found all over Britain in both gardens and the wider landscape, and it becomes clear that plant collecting has a wide and popular appeal. Even in countries like those of North America and southern Europe, a rich native tree flora has failed to quell the urge to gather and cultivate exotic and unusual species from far and wide.

Almost anywhere in the world where humans have lived, they have added to the naturally occurring list of plants. The earliest records of tree collecting involve species that were valued for their food or medicinal uses. As early as 1495 BC, during the reign of Queen Hatshepsut, Egyptian collectors were sent on a mission to Somalia to obtain incense trees (*Commiphora myrrha*) for growing back home. Movement of people during periods of conflict and conquest has inevitably been accompanied by transfer of plants as reminders of home as well as "trophies" of victory, and to allow the occupants of the newly conquered land to use their tried and tested crop plants. During their conquest and occupation of northern Europe, the Romans took with them many of their favourite plants including sweet chestnut (*Castanea sativa*), a tree valued for its wood as well as its bountiful harvest of nutritious nuts. In the British Isles, the species has since spread to become a common feature of woodland and park, accepted as an honorary native. Mediaeval crusaders returning from the Holy Lands between the 11th and 13th centuries brought back with them a bounty, not just of inanimate objects but also of new and exciting plants, including the now familiar, black mulberry (*Morus nigra*). Movement and collection of plants have also resulted from more peaceful occupation. Throughout mediaeval times, monks were among the most active cultivators of non-indigenous plants, and their well-developed networks of exchange were effective means of spreading the plants they favoured.

Gradually, during periods of peace and affluence, ornament joined function as a worthy reason for seeking and cultivating new plants. The discovery and subsequent colonisation of North America led to a great rush in plant introductions back to Europe during the mid 17th to early 18th centuries, and many of the early trees to cross the Atlantic were ornamental species including the tulip tree (*Liriodendron tulipifera*), black walnut (*Juglans nigra*), and red maple (*Acer rubrum*). Over the following 150 years the colonising Europeans sent back a steady flow of new plants from North America, culminating in their arrival at the great coniferous treasure troves of the western mountains and seaboard. Species like Douglas fir (*Pseudotsuga menziesii*) and coast redwood (*Sequoia sempervirens*) would soon become a regular feature of both forest and ornamental landscapes of Europe. (PLATE 2)

Other species followed from South America and Asia, all eagerly received by wealthy plant growers hungry for new and novel trees to adorn the grounds of their elegant houses. Robert Stayner Holford, creator of Westonbirt Arboretum in Gloucestershire, for example, paid the massive sum of 25 guineas each in the 1850s for a share in some of the first monkey puzzles (*Araucaria araucana*) to become available. Nursery companies sprang up with growing catalogues of plants to tempt their customers. Some, like the famous Veitch Nursery, even employed their own band of intrepid plant hunters to brave the hazards and deprivations of overseas expeditions to bring back the botanical treasure that would make them wealthy men. At the same time, back in England, John Claudius Loudon, the influential and longtime exponent of tree growing, was encouraging Victorians to plant and collect trees for both ornament and science. In 1835, the first volume of his great work *Arboretum et Fruticetum Britannicum* was published—a kind of call-to-arms for landowners to grow more and a wider variety of trees. This landmark publication eventually grew to eight volumes, covering not just the tree species themselves but their cultivation and layout, too. It received rave reviews, particularly from the affluent estate owners at whom it was primarily aimed. (PLATE 3)

But it wasn't just private tree growers who rode this tide of newly introduced species and the spirit to plant trees. Civic pride, combined with philanthropic funding from wealthy benefactors, allowed the establishment of a number of public urban arboretums during this period. The first was in 1840 in Derby, where Loudon was commissioned to design an arboretum for the industrialist Joseph Strutt, to be given to the City for public recreation. Loudon stated the aims of the arboretum to the Town Council as follows: "The Derby Arboretum would not only serve as a source of recreation and instruction to the inhabitants of Derby, and its neighbourhood, but as a standard of nomenclature to that part of the country generally; the collection of trees and shrubs being one of the most extensive ever planted, and the whole having been named with a degree of correctness scarcely to be found in any other garden." Other arboretums soon followed in Nottingham, Ipswich, and a number of other English cities.

By this time, North America was no longer just a supplier of plants to Europe. Increasingly, American gardens were benefiting from the botanical acquisitions arising from exploration elsewhere in the world. Public arboretums as well as private gardens were flourishing and providing an almost insatiable demand for new plants. Some even combined private ownership with public access, a trend that became common in the USA. One such was the Haverford College Arboretum, founded in 1835 outside Philadelphia. Its position within the overall college campus landscape was to become a popular model for subsequent American arboretums. But as in Europe, there was also a move to create civic arboretums for public recreation and learning. The most famous of these, Boston's Arnold Arboretum, would become a great public institution with its own collectors whose success made them revered figures in the world of botany. Among them was Englishman Ernest Wilson, who already had a proven track record of plant hunting for Veitch Nursery when he was attracted to work for the Arnold by its influential director Charles Sargent. He gained the nickname "China" Wilson from his three expeditions to that country between 1900 and 1910, during which he collected over a thousand plant species. (PLATE 4)

Today's tree collectors

Even today, tree collections continue to be established. Their diversity reflects the wide range of people and institutions behind them—from the new generation of private tree lovers, with a little bit of space and time, to public institutions like schools, colleges, and local authorities. Each has its own motivations and visions of what it wants to create as well as widely differing resources and constraints. What may seem out of the reach of individuals may be achieved by small community groups. Local parks or even street trees may be turned into a collection and become a valuable resource for learning and pleasure. New trees may be planted round the village green or cemetery to mark an event or centenary. Why plant just one species when there's the opportunity to create a small collection? (PLATE 5)

All these modern-day tree planters enjoy a wider range of plants than ever before on which to draw, and new techniques in propagation and arboriculture are making the art and science of tree growing ever more sophisticated and rewarding. Once the privilege of the landed rich and large institutions, the increasing availability and accessible pricing of nursery plants allow more people than ever to participate, even if on a very moderate scale. Plants that would have cost a small fortune when first introduced by 18th- and 19th-century plant hunters are now grown in large numbers and can be bought for very reasonable prices. And for those with an interest in propagation as well as collection, the possibilities for "growing your own" add another element of challenge and opportunity. Although the frantic pace of plant introduction has slowed, botanists continue to "move the goalposts" as their understanding of plant relationships develop and, once in a while, a new tree-treasure is discovered, sending a ripple of excitement through the dendrological world. One such was dawn redwood (*Metasequoia glyptostroboides*), known only from fossils until its discovery in 1941; it has since enjoyed a meteoric rise in fortune and become a common sight thanks to tree growers all over the world. Even more recently, in 1994, *Wollemia nobilis* (Wollemi pine) was discovered in a remote gorge in southeastern Australia. The wild population of this ancient tree is thought to be less than 100 individuals, but this figure is already far outnumbered by cultivated plants bought by modern collectors. Some of the purchase price they pay is contributing to conservation efforts to help secure the species' future.

With growing concerns over the effect humans are having on the planet, and in particular global climate change, trees and shrubs have become important indicators of and perhaps protectors against some of the effects of change. Their planting and cultivation has never been so important, and nowhere is this more so than in collections in which they can be recorded, studied, and compared. It would be a sad world where trees can be seen only in gardens and arboretums, but these can play an important role in reminding us all of the wild forests from which trees originally come.

The aim of this book is to provide inspiration and guidance to those setting out on the road of tree collecting. For those with modest ambitions, some of the information may be unnecessarily detailed, but it is hoped that however large, small, complex, or simple your vision may be, the following pages will help you to find answers to problems you may encounter along the way.

2 ▲ Getting Started
Planning and Establishing a Tree Collection

M any people have the idea to plant a collection of trees. The inspiration may come from a visit to an arboretum or a long-held interest in trees. But knowing how to take the idea forward is not always easy, and managers of arboretums around the world receive many enquiries from people seeking advice on the best ways to go about it. These enquiries may come from individuals or groups, some wanting to pursue a private interest and others hoping to create a public facility. Some have a clear idea of what they want to achieve, but many just have a simple love of trees and the instinctive desire to create something lasting and beautiful.

Establishing a private tree collection or arboretum on land that is already owned may be a relatively simple matter, provided sufficient funds are available and no major additional built features or roads are planned. Careful planning and design will still be needed, but the process of land purchase, gaining permissions, and fundraising may be unnecessary, allowing planting to be started fairly quickly. But for many people, the aim is to create a collection for reasons beyond private interest and pleasure. If the aim is to create an arboretum for public or institutional benefit, the process of establishment is likely to be a far more complicated matter. Apart from the practical aspects of site preparation, planting, etc., there will be a need to set up an organisational structure to guide the process and ensure the collection has a secure future. Before actual work can begin, a number of decisions will have to be made that will have a lasting and profound influence on the nature and management of the collection. In particular, it is important to determine a clear philosophy or "reason for being" that can be communicated to others. Initial ideas will have to be developed and described through plans and policies that may form the basis of applications for funding or planning permission. Support may be needed from individuals or groups, particularly those with skills not possessed by the original instigators. Only when all these hurdles have been jumped can effort turn to ground preparation, plant acquisition, and planting.

The origins of tree collections—little and large

A collection of trees and shrubs may begin in many ways and from a number of starting points. Perhaps the most important distinction is between those begun by individuals for their own interest and those that result from group effort for more public benefit. The former is a model that has a long and distinguished history. It may be assumed that this individualistic way of establishing a tree collection is one confined to those lucky individuals with a large garden, and it's certainly true that the choice of species and potential collection size grows with the area of land available. But even small urban gardens of a few square yards can accommodate a collection of shrubs of suitably modest size, particularly if grown in containers. More substantial suburban gardens can usually accommodate somewhat larger species, perhaps including a small to medium-sized tree or two accompanied by a mix of smaller shrubs. These modest collections may simply contain plants chosen on the basis of personal interest or aesthetic taste. More botanically inclined owners may choose to specialise, and some gardens of this kind go on to become holders of national collections. (PLATE 6)

On a larger scale still, many arboretums originally begun as private ventures have gone on to become great public institutions with a wider remit than that envisaged by their original creators. Many of the oldest arboretums in the USA were established by wealthy industrialists with a love of trees and a desire to leave a lasting legacy for later generations. The Morton Arboretum in Lisle, Illinois, and the Holden Arboretum near Cleveland, Ohio, are good examples. Although originally created for personal interest, arboretums like these have gone on to become places for public use and scientific study. Endowments now provide the core funding for these and many other collections, with additional income deriving from visitor charges, subscriptions, retail facilities, and bequests. Appointment of a board of directors or trustees is the usual way that these funds are administered to ensure that the original aims are pursued. (PLATE 7)

But not all established collections were begun by individuals for their own use. Many originate from collective effort and with a variety of organisational models. The roots of this kind of arboretum lie in a desire to create places for public recreation and learning. In the UK, citizens of some large cities are lucky enough to inherit civic arboretums, established in the 19th century. Like their American counterparts, the administrators of these institutions are often supported by loyal groups of members, or Friends, who provide financial help or lobby their political representatives on behalf of the arboretum. But large, prestigious collections like these are few and far between and beyond easy or regular travelling range of most of the population. They can, though, provide inspiration for more modest collections, established by and for local communities or interested groups. Local arboretums of this kind can become valuable additions to the landscape and provide an opportunity for people to enjoy and learn about trees and related environmental subjects closer to home. And tree collections don't have to be started from scratch. It may be possible to turn an area of land with existing trees into an arboretum fairly quickly and with little financial outlay.

Diverse collections for new needs

Like their well-established counterparts, new tree collections and arboretums can come about in various ways and to serve different purposes. Many cities and even smaller towns already have publicly financed gardens where trees and shrubs provide a backbone to the planting. Although most of these are not true collections since they are unlikely to have plans for what kinds of trees to grow and their recording, they do provide many functions of a collection and could, with relatively little effort in recording and labelling, be developed into such. Collections started in this way combine elements of both municipal park and botanical garden and continue a long tradition, beginning with public arboretums such as Derby in the UK. Even towns without public gardens often have the beginnings of a potential arboretum in the form of urban greenspace with trees. The infrastructure of paths and fencing is likely to be in place already and perhaps even a planned program of maintenance. Thinking even more broadly, nearly all communities, however small, have street trees maintained privately or by local authorities. These fragmented populations of trees may not immediately be considered as collections but, like those in parkland, often contain a number of different species, arranged in a way that makes them easily accessible by large numbers of people. Additional planting with a wider variety of trees and some interpretation and labelling can quickly give them a new dimension for providing information and learning. (PLATE 8)

Trees have, for centuries, been planted to commemorate events or people. Many small towns and villages planted commemorative trees to mark the turn of the third millennium, and most were identified with a plaque or label. In the Herefordshire town of Leominster, UK, National Tree Week of 2002 was marked by planting a ring of fourteen trees around the town. The Leominster Loop is a tree acrostic, the initial letters of the trees spelling out the project's name: lime, elm, oak, maple, etc. (PLATE 9)

Cemeteries often contain interesting selections of trees planted among the man-made memorials to add to the atmosphere of peace and permanence. The trees may even become the dominant symbol of remembrance. The National Memorial Arboretum in Staffordshire, UK, was established in 1997 to commemorate and celebrate those who have given their lives in the service of their country. The arboretum covers about 150 acres of reclaimed gravel and sand pits donated by the aggregate company who previously worked them. Over 50,000 trees have been planted in various arrangements from intimate memorial groups to grand sweeping avenues. Sometimes the species of trees has been chosen to add significance to the planting and provide poignant interpretation. A group of eucalyptus, for example, has been planted to acknowledge the vital role played by Australian airmen based in the UK during World War II. (PLATE 10)

Many schools and even hospitals have attractive grounds that may or may not contain trees. The potential educational and therapeutic benefits of developing a tree collection in these situations are great. In many countries, the perception of a growing alienation between children and nature has led to a movement to break the boundaries between school classrooms and the outdoor environment. "Forest classrooms" have become a popular way to teach children about trees and other aspects of the natural world. They may be bespoke teaching facilities established within forests or simple learning areas with benches within a wooded area of a playground. In either case, study of the trees and shrubs can be incorporated into and benefit various areas of the curriculum from maths through science to art and design. (PLATE 11)

Universities and colleges can also gain from establishing a tree collection. A good example is that at Keele University in Staffordshire, UK. Established in 2001, the arboretum was set up with clear educational objectives, not just to provide a resource for scientific study but also to address contemporary issues of public access, the environment, and social inclusion. The first step was to incorporate existing trees present on the university site and, after determining a list of suitable species, complement them with new planting. (PLATE 12)

Scientific collections like these can also be used to display or trial species or varieties suitable for local climatic or other physical conditions, thereby contributing to knowledge about their adaptability or potential for wider planting. Like other arboretums in the USA, the Arnold Arboretum has broadened its traditional scientific mission to seek a wider audience. It has embraced new concerns about sustainability by developing new reference collections for homeowners and urban designers. Their Leventritt Garden is a living laboratory and showcase for environmentally friendly gardening, including display of trees and shrubs tolerant of drought conditions. Inspirational examples like this can provide a lead for smaller groups looking for a modern relevance for newly created or old collections. (PLATE 13)

Organisation—cooperation, partnership, and public involvement

We have seen that arboretums arise from different origins and can serve a variety of purposes. But for any tree collection, and particularly a public one, a degree of cooperation and collective effort is likely to be needed to guide and move the establishment process forward. Some of these organisational models provide the opportunity for groups and communities to work together to plant trees for public benefit. These groups may acquire an open area of land and plant it with the species chosen, or take responsibility for an area with existing trees. In the latter case, the collection gets a head start, particularly if those trees help fulfil the collection's landscape, educational, or botanical objectives.

The original idea for a tree-planting project often comes from an interested individual or small group, but however knowledgeable and motivated the original instigators of the arboretum idea are, they are unlikely to have all the skills needed to take the project from idea to reality. Support may come from other individuals who can be persuaded to join the project or by "selling" the idea to an existing group with a natural interest or association with it. Gardening clubs or conservation groups are natural allies and are likely to have, among their members, people with useful knowledge when it comes to plant acquisition and establishment. Rotary and Kiwanis Clubs, civic trusts, and other benevolent organisations may also regard the establishment of an arboretum as a means of raising awareness for their work, generating community spirit, or providing volunteer opportunities for local people. As with individuals, the chance to leave something that will remain and grow long after its original creators have moved on is an attractive idea for groups like this, and their support may also help when it comes to gaining planning permission. Among their members there are also likely to be some with valuable experience of fundraising and other useful areas, while other members may, in the future, become committed members or Friends of the arboretum and provide continuing support long after the initial establishment phase.

Sometimes interested individuals get together to form tree groups dedicated to the recording and preservation of their local trees. In the UK, the Tree Warden scheme is a well-established national initiative enabling people to play an active role in conserving and enhancing their local trees and woods. Tree Wardens are volunteers appointed by parish councils or other community organisations who gather information about their local trees. They may also map their trees and record factors such as size and health. Some communities may be close to a university or college with a department relevant to the cultivation and study of trees. In return for some influence in the planning of the arboretum and subsequent access for study purposes, educational establishments like these may be willing to provide expertise and even some funding for the collection's establishment. Schools and colleges themselves may want to establish a tree collection for the obvious benefits that it may bring for educational and aesthetic reasons. Teachers, parents, or even governors may initiate the idea, taking advantage of the influence and organisational capacity of the Parent Teacher Association to take the project forward.

Some tree-planting projects are part of wider initiatives to improve the environment, particularly in urban situations. In the UK, Trees for Cities is an independent charity working with local communities to tackle global warming, create social cohesion, and beautify cities through tree planting. As well as greening the streets with new trees, the charity's various programs include community education projects and training initiatives to develop skills in horticulture and arboriculture. Their projects also include restoration and replanting of derelict public parks and gardens. (PLATE 14)

Independent groups may link their tree-planting plans to national initiatives such as Arbor Day in the USA and National Tree Week in the UK. Publicity and resources from these and other initiatives can add weight to even the smallest local project.

The planning group

Whatever organisations are formed or associations made in the process of starting a tree collection, the best course of action is usually to establish a planning or action group. This group will take the project through the various stages of planning and establishment. It may also become the management team for the collection post-establishment, and it is therefore important that the group should include individuals with the skills needed to accomplish the various tasks required. Of course, knowledge of trees and plant collections will be valuable, but skill in other areas such as planning, accountancy, and project manage-

ment should not be overlooked. Where specialist skills are needed, the group will also need to seek advice from outside experts. In the early stages, this may include technical questions concerning site suitability, surveying, or legal considerations. But first of all, the group will have to consider the feasibility of the original concept. Does the idea have any chance of success as it stands, or does it need to be reconsidered and modified in scope or nature? It will also be important for the group to begin to define the sequence of action required and a means of monitoring progress. To do this, it is useful to consider the establishment of the collection as a project with various phases along the way to completion. Figure 1 shows the phases that are likely to be involved. Project managers often use diagrams such as this to give an overview of a project's so-called life cycle and provide a means of identifying key components in the plan as well as establishing a timeline for progress.

As the project passes through the various phases of establishment, it is the job of the planning group to control the process. This may include checking that certain things have been completed before approving funds or giving the go-ahead to move to the next phase.

Throughout the project, the group will also need to communicate with the community in which the collection is sited as well as agencies from whom permission or funding may be required. To help with this, an initial concept plan may be produced indicating, in an attractive and simple way, the general outline of the project. The plan may be communicated via a Web site or on a leaflet or exhibition boards displayed in the most effective places. This may also be the first opportunity to invite interested parties to join the project through membership or donation. An annual subscription may be charged to raise funds and a newsletter produced to keep members informed about progress.

Planning—From Concept to Master Plan

Once a planning group has been established and the general concept agreed, the real work of planning the collection can begin. At this stage, the intentions are likely to be lacking in detail but at least the general objectives should be clear. Whether starting out with an open area

FIGURE 1. PROJECT LIFE CYCLE FOR ESTABLISHING A TREE COLLECTION

PROJECT PHASES

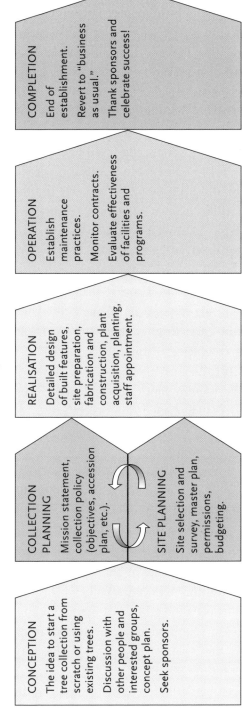

CONCEPTION

The idea to start a tree collection from scratch or using existing trees.

Discussion with other people and interested groups, concept plan.

Seek sponsors.

COLLECTION PLANNING

Mission statement, collection policy (objectives, accession plan, etc.).

SITE PLANNING

Site selection and survey, master plan, permissions, budgeting.

REALISATION

Detailed design of built features, site preparation, fabrication and construction, plant acquisition, planting, staff appointment.

OPERATION

Establish maintenance practices.

Monitor contracts.

Evaluate effectiveness of facilities and programs.

COMPLETION

End of establishment.

Revert to "business as usual."

Thank sponsors and celebrate success!

of land or developing a collection from existing trees, the importance of planning cannot be overstated. Without plans, progress will be haphazard with impulsive decisions leading to waste of time and resources and no guarantee that the end result will be what was originally hoped for. Plans are also a means of communicating intentions to other people and, since tree growing is a long-term venture, future managers.

The process of planning a tree collection is no different to that followed in most other disciplines. It should begin by defining the overall purpose of the collection, then, through various stages, describe how this will be achieved in practice. These plans will be of various kinds, from broad and aspirational to specific and detailed. At the highest level, they will be used to refine the concept of the proposed collection: why is it being established, what are the overall objectives, and who will benefit? Technical design plans showing the layout of the arboretum—including buildings, roads, interpretive facilities, and other features—will be derived from these overall principles and objectives. Both these areas of planning require considerable thought and a variety of skills. They may be carried on simultaneously, though some elements will need to be completed before others. Decisions made in one area will undoubtedly influence others, with adjustments to each along the way. For example, gaining much-needed financial support may require certain objectives to be included in the collection plans, while the need for easy public access to achieve educational aims could have an influence on choice of location.

It may be useful when considering the sequence of activity during the establishment of a collection to differentiate between the two distinct, but interrelated areas of planning. Collection plans are those that define the reasons for the collection itself, its objectives, and how the choice of trees and their arrangement will achieve them. Site plans are more practical and spatial in nature and show how the intended built and natural features of the arboretum will be designed and laid out. The latter also includes the process of selecting a site and assessing its suitability and any requirements for change or improvement. Throughout the process, these plans will provide the basis for gaining support and permission for development. As plans evolve, the planning group will need to meet regularly to monitor progress as well as consult other advocates, planning authorities, and specialists. The next stage in establishment is the actual implementation (or realisation) of the plans: laying paths and roads, constructing buildings and other structures, and, of course, planting the trees.

Setting the Course—Collection Planning

Some collections start almost by accident and only fairly late in their development become acknowledged as such. Others may have carried on for years without any documented direction or objectives, often maintained by a strongly motivated individual or small group. Even in these cases, it is never too late to define clear objectives and write a set of plans and policies. Doing so may even provide the impetus for restoration or growth. The nature and complexity of these documents will vary, just like the collections themselves, but all should be sufficiently accessible to those involved in support, development, and maintenance.

Mission statement

Planning a collection is not simply a matter of deciding what to grow and how to lay it out. It needs to begin by defining a mission or philosophy that can be referred back to at all stages in its development. You wouldn't design a building without knowing what it was to be used for, and the same is true of a tree collection. Why do you want to collect trees? The answer to this question will have a profound influence on all aspects of the venture from accession right through to the buildings and other facilities that may be needed. The mission statement therefore needs to encapsulate the essential flavour of the collection, both physical and cultural. This may seem rather grand for a small private collection of a few trees or shrubs with little or no public role, but even here, a short statement describing the purpose of the venture is likely to become a valuable reference source. Even the discipline of sitting down to write a statement may reveal a lack of clear direction where there was previously assumed to be one.

For more ambitious ventures where public benefit is intended, the mission statement will be an important means of communicating what may be fairly complex objectives in a simple and inspirational way. This is especially important where external funding or public support is being sought. In some situations, such as large urban municipal parks, the tree collection may be part of a larger establishment and the mission may be broader, with the trees contributing to a wider set of objectives. Walking, cycling, and many other activities, including appreciation of the trees, may coexist and make up the overall atmosphere of the area. In this case the mission statement for the tree collection may draw influence from and contribute to the wider mission for the recreational facilities of the city in which the park or other greenspace is situated.

Consultation. Since the purpose of a mission statement is to guide development and management of a collection, it is important that those involved in that process are consulted from the start in its writing. A mission determined from above and delivered to staff or other interested parties as a fait accompli is unlikely to promote a sense of ownership. On the other hand, an attempt to include every individual's particular priorities will be wordy and confusing, with the simple message lost in the detail. A middle line needs to be adopted with all opinions being sought and considered but with the planning group given the job of producing a representative but usable finished product. How wide this net of opinion-seeking is spread will vary from one situation to the next. It should certainly include those people whose jobs and livelihoods are (or will be) involved. The views of any benefactors or funding bodies should also be sought, as well as those with previous knowledge of collection establishment and management. Tree collections often rely financially and practically on the support of loyal followers, and it is particularly important that these natural allies are given the opportunity to have a say in the writing of such an important statement. For projects organised at a community level, consultation meetings may be organised with a presentation by one or more members of the planning group.

Mission content. The fundamental requirement of a mission statement is to define what the collection is there to achieve. As stated in the introductory chapter, this may be as simple as providing enjoyment and interest for the creator. On the other hand, it may be fulfilling a number of functions, possibly with potential conflicts, and the mission may be the first point at which priorities are defined. The length of the statement will vary depending on the complexity and breadth of the objectives to be met, but it should be remembered that this is a tool for communicating ideas, and an overlong statement is likely to lose the interest of readers and lack the essential ability to inspire. It's best to resist the temptation to put in more detailed objectives at this stage and instead describe these in the next level of planning. An example of a concise but descriptive mission statement is that of the Sir Harold Hillier Gardens and Arboretum, Hampshire, UK. A single inspirational sentence gives just enough detail as to what plants will be grown and why: "The Hillier Arboretum's mission is to enhance the understanding and enjoyment of the arboretum and to develop its horticultural, botanical, aesthetic, educational and conservation potentials, and to bring together as complete a collection of all those woody plants that can be grown in the temperate world without protection."

By stating the intention of growing woody and temperate plants, the statement is also, to some extent, setting boundaries. This may be an important purpose of a mission statement in order to focus activity in the intended areas. The statement also identifies the educational purpose of the collection, a theme that is developed in the mission statement of the Arnold Arboretum. Its mission is more detailed and begins to describe methods of delivery:

▲ to develop, curate, and maintain a well-documented collection of living woody plants from around the world that are hardy in the Boston area;
▲ to study these plants and their relatives and associates in nature through the maintenance of a herbarium and library and through directly related research in botany and horticulture;
▲ to provide instruction in botany, horticulture, dendrology, and other fields related to the living collections. (PLATE 15)

The National Arboretum at Westonbirt, Gloucestershire, UK, is owned and managed by the Forestry Commission and has a broad public remit that includes leisure, health, and learning. It has adopted a very brief and loosely defined mission statement in recognition of this diverse role: "To connect people with trees to improve the quality of life." This succinct approach has the benefit of being catchy and easy to remember. It also allows great scope for interpretation as to what activities contribute to it, a feature that can have the disadvantage of lacking guidance and allowing "mission creep." However, this can be overcome by clearer definition in an accompanying list of objectives or activities to be followed in pursuit of the mission.

Another short mission statement is that of the Holden Arboretum: "The Holden Arboretum connects people with nature for inspiration and enjoyment, fosters learning and promotes conservation." As with Westonbirt's mission, no attempt is made to go into the details of how these aspirations will be fulfilled.

The mission of the National Arboretum of New Zealand at Eastwoodhill gives a little more detail and broadens the aim to encompass nature more generally: "To foster understanding and appreciation of nature by education, research and enjoyment of our unique plant collection."

Setting objectives

Once a mission statement has been written, the next level of planning should aim to describe how the mission will be achieved, both in terms of the various objectives derived from it and the activities or programs that will be followed. As was just seen, some mission statements go some way to define the specific objectives for collections. But for most, these objectives are distinct from the mission itself, though they depend on it for their direction. For many simple private or community collections, they may be few and straightforward, but even here, consideration may reveal an opportunity to contribute to more than the basic purpose originally envisaged. Large or publicly owned collections will have a more complex range of objectives that may be derived from the overall aims of a larger organisation such as local government, charitable trust, or school. They may include things like public access, recreation, and learning as well as the development and maintenance of the tree collection itself. The following are the most common objectives for tree collections:

▲ science and research
▲ education
▲ landscape and recreation
▲ conservation
▲ historic preservation

Most collections will identify with at least two of these objectives. Their relative importance will change from one collection to another, depending on the interest of the collector or the nature of the institution. They may also give a local flavour to reflect climatic, cultural, or botanical factors. An example of this comes from the Waite Arboretum, Adelaide, Australia, where the list of three objectives includes research, learning, and leisure:

▲ to demonstrate and evaluate the suitability of a wide range of Australian and exotic trees to the local environment;
▲ to maintain, document, and develop the collection as a valuable resource for teaching and research;
▲ to provide an attractive and informative area for passive recreation with guided walks and interpretation material to enhance the enjoyment of visitors.

The Holden Arboretum has five objectives:

▲ acquiring, displaying, and maintaining documented horticultural collections;
▲ offering educational programming on plants and nature, emphasizing environmental stewardship;
▲ conducting scientific research on plants and ecology and disseminating research results;
▲ engaging individuals with the natural world to enhance fundamental learning, wellness, and health;
▲ conserving natural areas and protecting green space and sensitive ecosystems.

The lists of objectives for both the Waite and Holden Arboretums start to introduce some of the areas of activity that will be pursued. They thereby provide a translation from the mission's broad philosophy into specific practical programs. The mission statement of the Arnold Arboretum, given earlier, identifies three areas of activity: research, education, and horticulture. Further detail of how these activities will be pursued is described in other plans.

The process of defining objectives is an important one. Like the writing of a mission statement, it is essential to consult people with relevant knowledge and experience, as well as those involved in delivering results. Rather than just writing a list by instinct and previous experience, it's worth taking time to consider the whole range of potential objectives and whether the proposed or existing tree collection can distinguish itself from others by taking a new or innovative approach to meeting its mission. It is also important at this stage to be realistic: better to excel at meeting modest objectives than to fail to achieve unrealistic ones. It is a common mistake, for example, to try to grow a broader range of plants than the proposed site can support or the likely numbers of staff maintain.

Collection policy

Many plant collections describe their objectives and the plans and policies to deliver them in a collection policy. This document encapsulates both conceptual and practical elements of planning and provides the fundamental point of reference for the management and development of the collection. Having a written policy helps to provide continuity and maintain traditions and practices that may otherwise get lost over time and changes of staff. The document should also refer to the wider framework of legal, environmental, and ethical conventions within which the collection exists.

Most collection policies start by defining the collection's objectives before describing the scope and methodology for their practical delivery. They vary greatly in length, reflecting the relative complexity of the collections they represent. Some confine themselves to broad statements of policy, while others develop from these detailed practical prescriptions for various aspects of management, including specifications for planting, labelling, or arboricultural maintenance. To avoid an overlong and confusing document, however, it is usually best to keep practical guidance such as this as separate plans or appendices to the main policy. The collection policy itself should cover the following areas:

▲ objectives for the collection
▲ acquisition and accession of plants
▲ ethical policy and environmental standards
▲ collection management policy
▲ access policy

Acquisition and accession of plants. Few collections are likely to have enough land to grow more than a small proportion of the trees and shrubs available to the modern collector. Deciding what species or cultivars to collect and how to go about acquiring them are the two most important aspects of planning a collection of trees and shrubs. As well as determining the botanical content of the collection, choice of plants will also directly affect the eventual landscape of the arboretum and its suitability for the range of objectives pursued. Without clear written guidance it is all too easy to drift from the objectives of the collection, lured by easily obtained and superficially attractive plants rather than those that can make a real contribution to the mission. Clearly stated objectives should help to define the target range of plants to be accessioned but even so, written policy is essential in order to provide continuity and make best use of the land and maintenance resource available.

This subject of determining, describing, and implementing plans for plant acquisition is dealt with in more detail in Chapter 3, dedicated to plants.

Ethical policy. It is important to clearly state the collection's policy on the ethics relating to plant collection and cultivation. There may be occasions when managers will need to consider the implications of their activities and a written policy will provide the source of guidance. The most important potential area of concern is the impact of plant collecting on the wild populations from which they come and the sharing of the benefits of collection with the countries of origin. Where plants are being collected directly or indirectly from the wild or obtained from other collectors doing similarly, international conventions need to be adhered to and thorough records kept. The Convention on Biological Diversity (CBD) and the Convention on International Trade in Endangered Species (CITES) are the most important of these conventions. Their significance to plant collectors is described in more detail in Chapter 3.

Environmental standards. Tree collections by their nature may be considered to be environmentally beneficial. But they are not natural creations and require various kinds of maintenance to hold back the inevitable deterioration to disorder and jungle. As well as energy consumption, a variety of chemicals and materials may be used to keep the arboretum looking good and the trees safe and sound. The control of vegetation is a good example with everything from power mowers to herbicides used to keep grass and weeds at bay. Not only should all activities abide by legislation on environmental standards, but the collection policy should include a clear statement on the intention to minimise consumption and waste and describe any means to review and monitor these.

Collection management policy. The practical management of the collection, including techniques and work scheduling, is dealt with in Chapter 4. Trying to describe the detailed processes of maintenance in a collection policy will make it a complicated and overlong document, and it's usually best to stick to broad statements on overall principles of management at this stage.

Access policy. There are two main areas where it is essential to have clear policy on the level of access by others to the collection:

▲ Access for propagation purposes. There are many positive reasons for allowing other collectors or institutions to propagate plants in the collection. It may help to forge relationships with other arboretums or even contribute to safeguarding the future of an endangered species. On the other hand, care needs to be taken to ensure that the intended use of the resulting plants won't contravene ethical or other standards. Donors often ask that recipients of plant material agree to certain conditions, the most common being that they will not profit financially from the propagated plants. This is particularly important for plants originating in the wild, where the original permission to collect may have had a similar condition attached. The question of profiting from indigenous plants is an important component of the CBD.

▲ Access to information. One of the fundamental objectives of most tree collections is to improve understanding of the plants within them. In general therefore, collectors should share information about their plants with all interested parties. At the most basic level, this means publishing species lists but may also include more general information about the intentions for collection management and development. This information may be shared with other collectors through a plant network or more widely with visitors or Web browsers. The interpretive means by which this may be done are dealt with in more detail in Chapter 6. A statement of general policy including any areas of restriction on information—for example, on the location of endangered species—should be included in the collection policy.

Putting Things Together—Site Planning

The process of finding a suitable site for establishing a tree collection may be a long and difficult one. On the other hand, it may be as simple as gaining permission to put an area of publicly owned land to a slightly different use. For many collections where the site is already decided, the various stages of site selection will be unnecessary. Assessment of the proposed site will still be essential, however, and it is important not to accept the first area that becomes available without careful consideration of its suitability.

It may be useful to think of this planning process in three stages, though each could be broken into many smaller ones: site selection, site survey and assessment, and master plan.

Site selection

It goes without saying that the location in which a collection is to be established will have a direct effect on the possible range and kinds of trees that can be grown and the resources that may be needed to successfully establish them. But location is not just about the quality of the land and the aspect and climate associated with it. It may also be defined by its proximity to centres of population or ease of access and therefore have a direct bearing on the likely level of public usage and the potential benefits to the community. It is unlikely that the ideal site will be found to meet all the objectives for the collection, and a best-fit that meets all the important requirements is usually the most that can be hoped for. Some aims may have to be tempered to match the location, just as others will need to be downsized for budgetary reasons.

For many (and perhaps most) prospective tree collectors, consideration of location is an academic one only. Choice of site is not the issue but rather adaptation and utilisation of the area owned or available. For some sites, there may be existing public access and use for other activities, and it will be important to consider how compatible these will be if carried on alongside the tree collection. Public parks are a good example: in them, a range of sporting or other recreational activities may have a direct impact on any proposed tree collection.

Size. The objectives for the collection will, inevitably, give some idea of the area of land required for planting purposes and other intended programs. The range of species, their size, and the number of individual plants are all important considerations, and the accession plan will provide the main source of reference for these calculations. But areas may also be needed for access roads, buildings, and open areas, and these must also be considered before a realistic calculation of area available for actual planting can be reached. It is also important to remember that much of the total area may be unsuitable for certain purposes. Some existing habitats may be protected by law, while others areas may have unsuitable soil types or drainage. If part of the site is covered in woodland or other tree cover, a decision will have to be made: whether to replant it with collection plants or maintain it as shelter or a complementary landscape.

Climate. Rainfall and temperature patterns are, along with physical characteristics of the site, the most important factors determining its suitability for plant growth. Figures can usually be obtained from weather surveys carried out by government meteorological offices. It is important to consider not only averages but also extremes and their frequencies. It should also be remembered that climatic conditions and soil types are related issues—a water-retentive soil may, to some extent, offset poor rainfall figures, for example. The limitations imposed by rainfall levels or patterns may be judged by reference to the range of species grown in other arboretums with similar precipitation.

Physical characteristics. Although trees and shrubs vary in their requirements for good growth, choice of a poor site will greatly limit the range of species that can be grown successfully. Poor drainage, nutrient deficiency, toxicity, or other characteristics can make a site unsuitable for tree growth or greatly limit the range of species that can be successfully grown. On the other hand, trees are often grown on less valuable land, while more fertile areas are reserved for food crops. Sometimes, the only land available may appear fairly unpromising, but objective assessment could show it to be perfectly adequate.

Proximity to people. Plant collections are for people. Land in remote locations may be cheaper than that closer to town, but if provision of education and recreation are important objectives, opting for the former may be a false economy. Collections started in urban parks or even with street trees have a great advantage in this respect and have a head start when it comes to green credentials.

Site survey and assessment

Whether or not the proposed area of land is already owned, site assessment is likely to be required to judge its suitability for establishing a tree collection and any other programs intended to deliver the mission. Even where conditions are found to be suitable for plant growth, a survey may reveal other problems such as liability to flooding or planning restrictions that may make it unsuitable.

Before a thorough survey is carried out, a preliminary one may be commissioned. This may quickly identify major problems that make the site unsuitable or, where more than one location is being considered, eliminate the least suitable ones. Effort and money can then be dedicated to a more detailed survey of the chosen or best sites. A survey of this kind will require a specialist with knowledge of planning and, where appropriate, the range of existing habitats on the site. The result should be an accurate plan of the site showing all the elements of existing natural and artificial features. This plan will not only describe the site as it exists before establishment but also provide the base map upon which the master plan for the developing arboretum can be superimposed. It is important therefore that it is sufficiently detailed and includes the necessary information to be used for this purpose. The following features should be assessed during the survey:

- ▲ Boundaries. Accurately mapped with any physical markers (fences, walls, etc.) indicated.
- ▲ Topography. Major changes in land levels.
- ▲ Geology, soils, and water availability. Soil types, pH, fertility, water tables, liability to erosion, etc.
- ▲ Structures. Buildings, walls, bridges, etc.
- ▲ Roads and paths. The level of construction (surface material) should be described. Of particular importance will be public rights of way.
- ▲ Services. Gas and electricity lines, water pipes, and drains.
- ▲ Legal designations or protected features. Nature reserves, archaeological or historic features, etc. Description of status and level of protection may be necessary.
- ▲ Natural features. Rivers, lakes, rocky outcrops, etc.
- ▲ Natural habitats and vegetation types. Grassland, woodland, etc.
- ▲ Trees. May be plotted as notable individuals or as groups. A detailed tree survey may be carried out separately or as part of this overall site assessment. This will serve to identify trees worth retaining as well as their suitability for incorporating into the collection. Trees recorded at this stage may be numbered, plotted, and entered into the plant database (see Chapter 5, for more on cataloguing). Where anticipated development may involve removal of some trees, planning authorities may require a survey of this kind.

▲ Other constraints. Any other features that may limit the scope for development, for example, animal pests, or liability to flooding or subsidence.

As well as the graphic representation provided by the resulting plan, a written document describing other aspects of the site will be required. This should give more information about the various features shown and their suitability (or otherwise) for the proposed collection. It should also describe non-spatial aspects of the location, such as type and level of existing usage, proximity to population centres, or details of protected native species or habitats present.

Master plan

Once the collection's objectives have been clearly decided upon and the site assessment carried out, planning of the actual layout of the land area can begin. The master plan is a map that shows the intended spatial design of all the various elements of the arboretum. It therefore provides a vital link or "glue" between the two halves of the planning process: collection plans and site plans. The various elements to be shown on the master plan, including the collection itself as well as roads and other artificial features, will all contribute to the mission statement through the various objectives defined earlier. This is the point where the location or layout of any intended specialist or thematic collections may be planned. Great attention should be paid to getting these and other elements right. Not only will mistakes be expensive to rectify later, but poor layout may make it difficult to deliver interpretation or other objectives—badly planned walking routes that fail to lead visitors to information points, for example.

The importance of the master plan is not in its level of detail but in its graphical overview of all the arboretum's functions. More detailed plans will be produced later, with design of individual areas and features, but this plan is an important means of communicating overall intention. It will show, for example, the position and width of a planned road, but the actual specification for materials to be used will come later. Of particular importance is that the plan should show how the garden fits into its surroundings, including natural landscapes or urban features like roads or residential dwellings. An entrance road, for example, must come from somewhere, and this should be clearly shown. Arboretums vary greatly in the range of features they include, and this will be reflected in the complexity of the plan.

It is not only budding collections that can benefit from a master plan. Many well-established arboretums in need of redevelopment or renewal turn to the master plan as a way of planning and communicating their intended restoration. In these cases the plans will clearly show the changes to the existing collections and facilities.

The following is a list of the most important things to include in a master plan:

▲ site boundaries and interfaces with surrounding areas
▲ building and other areas to be developed
▲ other structures
▲ means of access and movement, including roads, paths, and other routes
▲ areas for collection planting
▲ areas of natural habitat

The level of detail and scale of the plan will depend on the size of the area and the range of features to be included. For very small areas with relatively small numbers of plants, prominent trees and shrub groups may be individually shown. For more extensive collections, the larger scale required may call for a less precise representation. In most cases it will be desirable to be able to reproduce the map on a single sheet of paper to allow it to be used for simple display and distribution. Increasingly plans are produced with computer design or mapping programs and converted into a document format that can be viewed on a personal computer. This has the great advantage of allowing plans to be easily copied and distributed by e-mail and published on a Web site. Even with this technology available, it is still desirable to keep the plan as simple as possible. Different features should be clearly labelled, and habitat types should be differentiated by coloured shading and described in a key. For more complex plans it may be necessary to provide a written document to accompany the plan and explain the elements within it. The most important function of this document is to explain how the various mapped elements shown on the master plan will contribute to the collection's objectives. It may also describe the means of transforming features of the existing site (shown on the site survey) to the condition shown on the master plan. For example, the plan may describe an intention to thin existing woodland to incorporate a new specialist collection of flowering cherries. Where a computer-based mapping system has been used for the initial site survey, useful themes such as boundaries, habitat types, and topographic features may be selected as background and overlaid with the master plan elements to be developed. (PLATE 16)

Planning consent. The master plan, once produced, is likely to be the fundamental reference for seeking planning approval. It is therefore important that the purposes of the various features are clearly indicated.

The level of permission required to establish a collection of trees and shrubs will depend on a number of circumstances. Countries and states or counties within them vary greatly in their planning laws and, in addition, local bylaws will need to be taken into consideration. It is rarely the actual tree planting that requires consent, but other features of the arboretum such as roads, buildings, and other built structures. The important thing is to inform planning authorities early in the planning process to avoid delays and expensive changes later on. The master plan will provide the main means by which plans can be communicated.

Design and Spatial Arrangement

The detailed design qualities of many of the elements shown on the master plan will require careful consideration. This is equally true of the collection(s) themselves as well as the buildings, roads, and other features. For arboretums relying on public admission charges and other onsite sources of income, it is important to remember that the layout and design will have the purpose of supporting the business as well as the tree collection itself. It may be important, for example, to provide an area close to the exit for a plant centre or other retail opportunities.

Another important influence will undoubtedly be the interpretive function of the arboretum and consideration of the layout from the point of view of the visitors' experience. This is covered in more detail in the section on interpretation in Chapter 6.

Artificial features

The design of the arboretum's artificial features will have a profound effect not only on its function but also on its attractiveness. Since it is the trees and shrubs themselves that represent the focus of any arboretum, it may be natural to regard built features as an intrusion or, at best, an inevitable necessity for providing access or other functional requirements. On the other hand, well-designed and carefully positioned features can minimise distraction from the beauty of the trees and even help to provide a structural framework to the arboretum and become attractive features in their own right.

The layout of paths, for example, must be carefully planned to allow easy flow of people to each area of the arboretum. But the materials from which they are made will also have an important influence on the aesthetic quality of the landscape. However well designed individual features may be, if they each have a completely different style or feel, the result will be visually disjointed. The same is true of other features, from waste bins to location signs and interpretive plinths, and it is important that attention is given to the detail of each. In particular, technical standards for features such as roads, car parks, and the like should be followed carefully. (PLATE 17)

The treescape

It goes without saying that the most important landscape component in an arboretum is that of the trees and shrubs themselves. To some extent the materials for this plant landscape—the various species and cultivars of trees and shrubs—will be determined by the criteria for deciding what will be grown in the collection through the accession plan. But their arrangement, and particularly whether or not they are to be planted systematically or in a more ornamental fashion, is key to the resulting treescape. Plans for small collections with relatively few trees and shrubs may be drawn at a sufficiently small scale to show the intended position of each one individually. But for most collections, the master plan is likely to be less detailed with planting shown only as areas. The question of planting layout and style may be left to a separate landscape plan. This subject is covered under its own heading later in the chapter.

Equality of access

Consideration for disabled visitors is an important part of planning the layout and design of the arboretum and its features. Many countries have statutory requirements to provide equal access to people with disabilities. At a basic level, this may mean designing paths with a suitable specification for wheelchairs, but there are many more subtle consequences, including positioning and clarity of signage. As well as meeting minimum standards for all facilities, arboretums can greatly enhance the value of their collections to disabled people by adapting their programs of interpretation, events, and publicity.

Realisation of the Master Plan

The realisation phase of establishment may be described in simple terms as the transformation of the site from its original condition (shown in the site survey) to that described by the master plan. In reality there are a number of smaller stages within the phase, including specific design of elements within the master plan as well as site preparation for both built and natural features. Actual planting and construction is the final stage before the project can be handed over to those who will manage the collection day to day. The management group will have to make the judgment on when plans are sufficiently complete to authorise their implementation. It is always tempting to get started on construction or planting as soon as possible, but mistakes at this stage can be very expensive and it is best to ensure that plans have been thoroughly considered and approved before this phase is given the go-ahead. Project managers often draw up a so-called implementation plan to show the project's various elements, their sequence, and resources required.

The subject of construction of buildings, roads, and other artificial features is not a suitable one for this book. Most individuals or community groups will, in any case, not need to be directly involved in this area of work, which should be strictly managed by qualified professionals experienced in the area of construction design and management.

Site preparation

Though little can be done to change the underlying soil type or prevailing climatic conditions, some measures such as drainage or fertilising can be taken to improve the situation for tree growth. However, in general, these tend to be expensive and no substitute for site selection (where possible) and realistic expectations for what species of trees can be grown in the ambient conditions. This is an area where collection planning must take into account the limitations imposed by the site.

On many unplanted sites, one factor to be considered will be exposure. In extreme cases this may make a site unsuitable, but it is more likely that some kind of shelter planting will be required. This plantation may be a separate feature, managed differently from the tree collection itself. In this case it could be considered a form of site preparation, particularly where establishment of a shelter belt is required before planting of the collection can proceed.

Arboricultural work

Where the site being developed has existing trees, arboricultural work is likely to be necessary to remove those considered unsuitable for inclusion in the collection due to their position, condition, or the species concerned. Even where trees are to be left and accessioned into the collection, they may require remedial pruning or other work. This subject is dealt with in more detail in Chapter 4, in the section on maintenance.

Planting

Planting is, perhaps, the defining element in the creation of a tree collection. For that reason it has the greatest potential for involvement of sponsors, partners, and members of the public. The techniques of tree planting are not difficult to master, and there is no reason why even inexperienced planters shouldn't be able to take part, provided a few simple rules are followed. As well as using the right planting techniques, it is important that careful consideration be given to spacing and arrangement so that plants, as they grow, can develop fully and be best appreciated. The technical aspects of tree planting and the continuing maintenance of young plants are covered in Chapter 4.

Plant Layout and Landscape Design

As described earlier in the chapter, the master plan should show and describe how the various landscape components of the arboretum will be laid out. This may include traditional landscape features—avenues, drives, rides, glades—that will rely heavily on planting for their definition. What the master plan is unlikely to do is indicate the finer details of plant layout and design. This level of planning is usually left to landscape designers and horticulturists with knowledge of the trees and their potential to contribute to the overall treescape. Their efforts should aim to create a landscape that contributes to the arboretum's own particular unique character or "sense of place." It may be influenced by wider historical or modern styles, but it should show a confidence to interpret them in a distinctive way. (PLATE 18)

In thinking about the options for laying out the plants in a collection, it is interesting to consider the most simple form of plant layout possible: forestry trees are often planted in single species plantations arranged in straight lines so that each tree has an appropriate and equal space. Few gaps are left except for roads and other practical purposes, in order to make the most of the land available. There's no reason why this model should not be followed by tree collectors, and it may suit the purpose of purely scientific collections where aesthetic considerations are not important. Species trials are often laid out in plots of this kind for easy maintenance and monitoring. But for most collections a degree of heterogeneity is desirable to make them more attractive. This is achieved by changing two aspects of the forestry plantation model: the species arrangement (mixing different species together) and spacing (planting at differing spacing, depending on plant size and the clumping effect desired). In addition, gaps can be left in the form of rides, glades, and vistas to provide contrast with planted areas and give clear views of the trees and allow appreciation of their stature. Manipulating these two aspects is, in a nutshell, what designing a treescape is all about. Appreciation can also be given to artificial features and topography, so that the plant and geographical and built components complement rather than conflict. Of course, there is almost infinite scope for invention and (thankfully) no two landscapes will be quite the same. (PLATE 19)

Landscape styles

To make sense of the range of landscaping possibility, we need to consider different landscape styles from regular to naturalistic. It is also important to understand the historical background to arboretum planting styles, since they may provide guidance for both existing and newly created collections. Indeed, for those collectors involved in restoration of an historic arboretum, adhering to the prevailing style is likely to be an essential requirement.

The traditional arboretum landscape. The history of the arboretum dates back to the late 18th and particularly 19th centuries. At that time the formal garden with its strict avenues and geometric beds was rejected in favour of more natural styles. In the UK, Lancelot "Capability" Brown and Humphry Repton were designing estate landscapes in which trees were valued for their aesthetic qualities. Initially these were native trees, but gradually, as they became available, exotic species were incorporated into these landscapes to provide additional interest. From the 1830s, private and public arboretums flourished and, despite influences encouraging systematic arrangements, most adopted more aesthetic and garden landscape principles to attract sponsors and visitors.

John Claudius Loudon, who designed the first public arboretum in Derby, advocated a Gardenesque style. His recommendation was to arrange trees and shrubs in such a way that each plant should be displayed to its full potential. The style was derived from the earlier Picturesque style, and the distinction between the two is often unclear. Both hark back to classical theories of landscape painting from the 17th century and aim to use trees, shrubs, and other natural features to create real landscape "pictures." Various principles were promoted such as variety, intricacy, and connection. The first of these was achieved by combining species with varying shapes, textures, and colours. Seasonal variety was also catered for using flowering and autumn-colouring species as well as others for winter interest. Evergreens such as yew and rhododendron were used to divide the landscape into smaller areas, thus providing intimacy and a sense of adventure. Winding paths guided visitors through the unfolding landscape in order to provide the optimum views, while clump planting provided the appropriate scale and a contrast to open grassy glades. (PLATE 20)

From the point of view of a plant collection, the important thing about these styles is that trees and shrubs are combined to complement each other aesthetically. Among the plants grown for their botanical, scientific, or educational value there are likely to be many others included for purely landscape reasons. Some of these may be recurrent species, planted to provide continuity or "connection" and a quiet contrast to more "exciting" ones. In planting styles of this kind, great sensitivity and skill is required to achieve the desired landscape effect without compromising each individual species' requirements for light and space. (PLATE 21)

Although these landscape styles date back to 18th-century England, their influence spread elsewhere, and the landscape principles behind them have stood the test of time. In the USA, the founders of the Haverford College Arboretum employed English landscape designer William Carvill to draw up the master plan for the campus. Carvill took the designs of Humphry Repton as his model, using the college buildings as the focal point for the planted avenues, lawns, and roads. A later example, dating back to the early 20th century, is the English Park at the Morris Arboretum in Philadelphia.

Even today, modern arboretum planters often adopt the traditional style—sometimes without knowing it. And at a much smaller scale, many private gardeners with more modest aspirations arrange their gardens in a similar way, albeit with shrub beds and lawns replacing large clumps and grassy glades.

New landscape styles. Despite the popularity of the 19th-century garden landscape, many arboretums adopt other styles, often in combination with or alongside, the more traditional ones. Some have continued down the naturalistic road; so-called forest gardens were an idea of the early 20th century but have gained popularity since. Arrangement of trees and shrubs is intended to mimic a natural forest structure with canopy and shrub layers and an intentionally unkempt look. This model may be well suited to geographical collections, where the intention is to give an impression of the native woody vegetation of a particular country or forest type. The lower requirement for maintenance also makes it an attractive option for collections with little resource for grass cutting and other aesthetic management operations.

Some arboretums have returned to more regular or formal arrangements. These may reinterpret traditional features such as avenues and allées or explore the possibilities of geometric planting. These designs can be used to create feature collections within a more irregular landscape. The Arnold Arboretum's Leventritt Garden (PLATE 13) is a good example of this approach. Collections designed with a national or cultural theme are another option. Japanese gardens are particularly popular, and by using dwarf cultivars or bonsai techniques, whole landscapes can be created in miniature. (PLATES 22 AND 23)

Landscape plans

Drawing up a landscape plan can be done in various ways. At one extreme, the plan may specify the position and species of every tree or shrub group. This may work for very small collections or historical landscapes where precise restoration or preservation is important. However, in most cases this approach is both impractical and overly restrictive, and a more flexible plan is better. For most collections a practical solution is to adopt a set of landscape principles that help guide plant layout and capture the atmosphere intended. These principles may be similar to those used by 19th-century landscapers (variety, connection, etc.) or adapted to a different style. The following paragraphs provide some examples of the kind of principles or rules that may be used to guide plant layout.

- ▲ Open space and spatial diversity. Plan the position and shape of open areas at an early stage. Consider the paths, rides, and other routes followed by visitors, and position trees accordingly. Use evergreen species to control views and create anticipation and visual intrigue. (PLATE 24)
- ▲ Grouping and scale. Group trees and shrubs according to the scale of the landscape. Single small trees or shrubs positioned in a large open landscape will look out of place and lost. Larger species or smaller ones planted as a group will look better. Where the intention is for groups of shrubs or trees to merge into one combined form, spacing of individual plants should be determined from the expected crown spread of the species concerned.
- ▲ Variety and contrast. Combine species that provide contrast. Grouping narrow or columnar trees with broad spreading ones results in an interesting skyline and emphasises their diversity. Different foliage colours and textures can be used in the same way. Remember that variety can also include seasonal change and the interesting (and sometimes unexpected) combinations it produces.
- ▲ Continuity and background. Avoid placing too many dramatic or accent plants together. Use them as highlights amongst more commonplace ones. Consider using background woodland or existing tree cover as a means of providing continuity between these more showy species. Where this is absent, a suitable recurrent species may be planted. This can provide a secondary purpose such as shelter or screening. (PLATE 25)
- ▲ Differentiation. Where possible allow different areas of the arboretum to acquire their own sense of place through distinctive species choice. This may develop naturally from soil or other physical variation or historical differences. Some areas may also be planted for a particular seasonal interest.

Funding the Collection

Most plant collections rely on a variety of funding sources for their establishment and subsequent development and maintenance. For people involved in fundraising for the initial establishment, the focus will be on securing the necessary funds to realise the various plans and activities anticipated. But the funding required for a tree collection is not confined to the establishment phase, and it is important even at this early stage to consider the ongoing costs of maintenance. There is, after all, little point in creating a wonderful arboretum if there is no means of looking after it. On the other hand, once established, the range of possible funding sources will increase, and these may be considered even at this stage. Individuals planting a simple garden collection may think they have a pretty good idea of how much it's likely to cost, but time spent preparing proper calculations may give unexpected results and avoid surprises! The costs of the trees themselves may be the obvious focus for budgeting, but protective cages, fencing, mulch, labels, and the occasional services of an arborist should not be overlooked.

For institutional or community collections, a detailed and objective means of budgeting is required, and this can be achieved through a financial or business plan. For most collections of this kind, public finance provides the basic funding, and it will be important for these plans to link funding to the objectives of the collection and demonstrate value for money. In many collections, there is likely to be a shortfall between direct funding and the money they require to fulfil their ambitions, and other sources of income should not be overlooked. The following headings describe the main sources of funding that may be available for a tree collection. Some kinds of funding are universally applicable to all phases of establishment and areas of activity, while others may be available only once the collection is up and running, or for identifiable projects. To make the most of fundraising opportunities, managers may need specific skills in this area of work in order to match areas of need to appropriate funding sources.

Public or institution grants

These grants typically come from a parent organisation, such as permanent endowments from trusts or other charitable owners. Local authorities or governing bodies of universities or colleges may also fulfil this role and award an annual maintenance grant, administered by an arboretum management group or committee. Although this kind of funding has the obvious advantage of security deriving from a long-term relationship between funder and collection, this income should not be taken for granted. Regular review of the arboretum's objectives and their contribution to that of the parent body is essential, particularly where the latter go beyond the collection itself. This may be the case where an arboretum is situated in a larger park or other public space. Proving value for money may require managers to evaluate the arboretum's public benefit through questionnaires or other means.

Grants of this kind are particularly valuable for providing secure funding for general ongoing costs, including staffing, materials, and maintenance.

Donations and subscriptions

Donations to both private and public gardens and arboretums provide a valuable source of income. These donations, whether one-off gifts or regular donations, may come from individuals or organisations. Many arboretums register as charities to take advantage of the tax and other benefits available for such organisations. Membership schemes or Friends groups provide an administrative framework for donations as well as a means of communicating with supporters. Membership is often linked to free admission and other benefits, such as discounts on purchases from retail outlets.

Project funding

Many kinds of funding bodies prefer giving money to definable projects with a clear start and end. As has been seen, the initial establishment of an arboretum may be described as a project in itself and therefore, with skilled fundraising, qualify for grants from these bodies, including commercial organisations, government agencies, foundations, lottery funds, etc. On the other hand, some organisations fund only very specific areas of work. Some, for example, may fund the educational aspects of a project but not built features, such as car parks or roads. It may therefore be necessary to break the overall establishment plan into smaller discrete sub-projects that can be funded separately.

Earned income

There is an enormous range of possibilities for arboretums to improve their financial position through earned income. These go well beyond the basic charge for admission and may even provide a means of keeping this charge at a lower rate than would otherwise be possible. Additional funds of this kind may also make the difference between basic economic survival and the ability to take on new activities through additional staff or other resources. If managed carefully, some sources of income can even enhance the arboretum's appeal to visitors or provide a means of interpretation. The danger of adopting a more commercial approach is that if money earning activities go too far or are inappropriate in nature, the fundamental purpose of the collection may become confused with its fundraising ones, and the arboretum may lose sight of its mission. It is vital therefore that commercial activity be carefully considered and, where possible, matched to the main objectives of the collection. Evaluating the suitability of any proposed activity of this kind must take into account its contribution to the arboretum's objectives and atmosphere as well as the expected financial costs and benefits. These are some of the possible means of earning income:

- ▲ Admissions charges
- ▲ Retail sales from shops and plant centres. Where these include sales of plant or wood products, display information may include messages about conservation or sustainability. This subject is covered in more detail in the section on interpretation in Chapter 6. (PLATE 26)
- ▲ Events. These may include purely commercial ventures that take

advantage of the site itself, or others with a link to the trees or collection. The former may include rock concerts or weddings; the latter, plant fairs or wood-craft shows. These more "relevant" kinds of events may be less profitable, but if they make some additional contribution to the collection's mission, any evaluation should take this into account. (PLATE 27)

▲ Courses and workshops. These may cover a wide variety of activities from green woodworking, through fungus forays, to making Christmas decorations from plant material. As with some kinds of events, their value as a means of promoting learning is likely to be at least as significant as (if not more significant than) their fund-raising potential.

▲ Tree adoption schemes. Many collections operate schemes by which individuals or groups can adopt a tree. These may be operated as a special kind of donation scheme, with the donor receiving acknowledgement of the gift through a named label or plaque on their tree of choice. Charges vary greatly, as do the means of recognising the donor's contribution. The danger is a proliferation of possibly unsightly plaques and additional administration that may come to outweigh the financial benefits. It is particularly important that schemes of this kind do not start to influence the choice of plants. They should support the accession policy rather than dictate it. For this reason, some arboretums provide donors with a list of existing trees suitable for adoption.

▲ Services provided, including advice and consultation given by staff professionals. Some institutional arboretums charge for tree advice through a special phone number service. Others offer consultancy services to companies and individuals.

▲ Sales of wood and other byproducts of maintenance.

▲ Sponsorship and royalties. Some collections receive support from commercial companies in return for endorsements or advertising space. This support may be given as cash payments or in-kind in the form of products such as tools or materials. Other income may derive from charges for use of the arboretum for photographic or other commercial uses.

3 ▲ The Trees
What To Collect and Where To Obtain Plants

For most people starting or managing a tree collection, the plants themselves are the real motivation, and the process of choosing what to grow is one of the most enjoyable and rewarding aspects of the venture. It may be the beauty of the leaves and flowers or the awe-inspiring physique that provides the excitement. Botanically minded collectors take a more intellectual interest by considering the relationships between the plants they want to collect and target particular groups. Whatever direction the collection takes, the process of choosing and obtaining plants is one that requires careful consideration and planning. For small private or "back garden" collections, this may simply be a question of thinking about how many trees can be accommodated in the available space and producing a list of desirable species. A blend of plants with different characteristics may be chosen to serve different landscape requirements and represent at least some of the main groups of trees and shrubs. If the collection is intended to be more than just a selection of personal favourites, gathered as and when they become available, there needs to be logic behind the process. Whatever the starting point—open ground or an area with existing trees—a rationale is needed to ensure that collecting is more than a random process of impulse buying and, as with all other areas of development, the mission statement and overall objectives should provide this direction. This chapter deals with the process of deciding what plants to collect and how to go about obtaining them. It should be remembered that plant collectors who have chosen to limit their attention to just trees and shrubs have already taken a major step in defining the scope of their collection. Further definition will serve to identify what should, and just as importantly what should not, be collected. Managers of large collections with complex or specific objectives usually prepare a written plan or policy to provide guidance in these areas. (PLATES 28 AND 29)

It will become clear that selection of plants is not just a question of choosing the right species or cultivars to meet the collection's aims. There are also decisions to be made about the source of plants: should they be obtained from commercial nurseries, from other collectors, or directly from wild populations? Horticultural considerations about the choice of the types of plants (bare-rooted versus container-grown, the most suitable sizes, selection, etc.) are also important and are dealt with later in the chapter.

Plant diversity and the language of plant collection

Inevitably, consideration of the plants to be included in a collection involves the classification and naming used to order and define them. Much of the content of this chapter therefore relates closely to the subject of cataloguing, dealt with in Chapter 5.

Before considering the choice of plants, it is useful to look at the way they are described and distinguished from one another. Like all plants, trees and shrubs are classified and named according to their relationships to one another in an attempt to bring some order and understanding to the world's arboreal diversity. Plant science is not a recent discipline, and a number of botanical documents dating from classical Greece and Rome describe the flora of the authors' native Mediterranean, as well as further afield. These early botanists were the first to begin the process of systematic description of the plants they saw and to ascribe definitive names to them. But these descriptions and names were far from consistently applied or used, and it wasn't until 1753, when Carl Linne published his book *Species Plantarum*, that modern plant classification was born. Linnaeus, as he has come to be known, gave order to the world of plants by placing them in families depending on their physical attributes. Naming (or nomenclature) reflected these relationships and allowed botanists, on discovering a new plant, to objectively name it according to its similarity to already known species.

It is important to remember right from the start that trees and shrubs are just large plants, and their botanical classification owes little to their physical size or structure. A large tree is quite likely to be more closely related to the tiny herbaceous plant growing unnoticed in the grass at its base than the similarly sized tree next to it. When deciding on the right plant "pigeonhole" in which to place a particular species, botanists are far more interested in the minute structure of flowers and fruit than the woody nature of trunk and branches. These anatomic details are an indication of a species' evolutionary descent and therefore its relationship to other species. Once determined, these plant relationships are represented by a hierarchy of classification that gradually sorts species into groups with increasingly subtle differences from one another. At the highest level, trees can be divided into flowering plants (angiosperms) and conifers and their allies (gymnosperms). Among the angiosperms, oaks can be separated from magnolias at an early stage, their flowers and fruits being substantially different. However it is only at the final level of classification that the species *Quercus rubra* (red oak) can be separated from its close relative *Q. coccinea* (scarlet oak). At an intermediate level, the relationship of both (and all other) oaks to beeches is shown by the inclusion of both groups in the same family—the beech family, Fagaceae. (PLATES 30 AND 31)

These various levels of classification are given different names to help define them—class, order, family, genus, species. For most people, the lowest three—family, genus, and species—are of most interest since they are those used from day to day as a means of ordering and describing plants.

Classification of the natural variability of plant life is an artificial discipline. Physical or geographical distinctions between species or populations of plants are often unclear and therefore open to debate. Individual plants of a single species may vary greatly from one another in their appearance over a small geographical area or even growing side by side. For this reason, botanists do not always agree on the correct classification or naming, and different schools of opinion adopt conflicting names. Even where agreement exists, progress in understanding plant relationships through greater research or technological advance such as DNA analysis leads to shifts in classification and corresponding nomenclature. Species may be amalgamated, split into two separate species, subdivided into subspecies, or even moved to new genera or families. Collectors need to be aware of this fluid nature of classification, not just to keep current with name changes but also to appreciate that developing a worthwhile collection is not simply a matter of gathering a large number of different species. Depending on the collection's objectives, the number and diversity of individuals of a single species may be equally (or more) valuable.

In addition to the diversity of wild plant life available from natural sources, centuries of human selection and breeding have "moulded" some plants into forms that meet practical needs or aesthetic taste. In some cases these cultivated plants end up looking very different from the wild-types from which they originate. The most obvious of these are the plants that meet our essential need for food and clothing. Apples and plums have both been subjected to careful selective breeding for centuries, resulting in cultivated forms that produce fruits of a size, flavour, and quantity to suit human need. During affluent times in human history, plants have also been selected and propagated for their colour, size, interesting shape, or other features that provide interest in the garden. These cultivated varieties, or "cultivars," provide collectors with an additional source of plants to be considered when deciding what should be included in the collection. Some species show a particularly broad natural variability that provides rich pickings for plant breeders looking for new and novel varieties. Japanese maple (*Acer palmatum*) is a good example, with over 800 cultivars to its name. It would, in theory, be possible to create a very colourful and diverse collection of trees containing just this one species! (PLATE 32)

Naming plants

It has already been stated that plant naming is linked to classification. It is also a means of describing the plant and a unique "label" to allow all botanists, collectors, or other interested parties to converse with one another with a confidence that they are discussing the same plant. Although many of us use common names to describe our local trees or ones that we are familiar with, care must be taken to avoid confusion. The same common name may refer to different species in different places, and a single species may have a number of common names used by different people. Tulip tree (*Liriodendron tulipifera*), for example, is also sometimes known as white poplar in its native USA even though it is unrelated to true poplars. (PLATE 33)

One of Linnaeus's great contributions to science was his so-called binomial plant naming. This simple system combines the genus and species elements of the name to provide the botanic name. *Quercus coccinea* brings together the genus name for oak (*Quercus*) and the species name (or epithet) for scarlet oak (*coccinea*). Although there are hundreds of other oaks and many other genera with the species epithet *coccinea* (*Crataegus coccinea*, for example), the combination of both is unique. Note that the genus name always begins with a capital letter, the species epithet with lower-case. The whole name is also written in italics or underlined to distinguish it from other text. When botanists decide that a species is sufficiently variable to subdivide it further, various terms are used, the most common being subspecies, variety, and forma. For example, Japanese maple is often divided into three distinct subspecies: *amoenum*, *palmatum*, and *matsumurae*. The full name then becomes *Acer palmatum* ssp. *amoenum*, etc.

Occasionally, in both natural and artificial (cultivated) conditions, closely related species may hybridise. The resulting hybrid taxon is identified as such by the insertion of an × between the generic and specific names. London plane (*Platanus ×hispanica*) is the result of hybridisation between the American buttonwood (*P. occidentalis*) and Oriental plane (*P. orientalis*) from southern Europe.

The standard reference for plant naming is the International Code of Nomenclature for Cultivated Plants (ICNCP), published by the International Society for Horticultural Science. This regularly updated code sets down the correct form of naming for both naturally occurring and artificially selected plants. Plants resulting from artificial selection are often given cultivar names to distinguish them from the wild-type plant and indicate their origin. The additional name is added to that of the species from which it originates but is given a capital letter and contained in inverted commas, though no italics or underline. *Acer palmatum* 'Osakazuki' is an old cultivar of Japanese maple.

These various names, derived from the elements of genus, species, etc., are the basic units of currency of any plant collection. Each unique plant type is referred to as a taxon (plural, taxa) and most collectors produce lists as a means of describing the scope and size of their collection. These names and some knowledge of plant classification may also provide collectors with a means of defining and describing the intended development of the collection. As plants are collected and added to the collection, a process known as accessioning, each new accession is allocated a unique number to differentiate it from others. This process is described in more detail in Chapter 5.

So what has all this to do with the practicalities of deciding what plants to grow in a collection of trees? Since the means of describing plant diversity is the names used to identify them, the process of defining what will be accessioned and planted will inevitably rely on their use along with an understanding of plant classification at their source. A collection of trees and shrubs is largely defined by the number and variety grown, and it is common to see them described in terms of the number of species or taxa they contain or the particular groups of plants represented. This is often seen as a measure of the botanical value of a collection, and certainly those recognised as leading collections tend to have an impressive range and number of species. But even the largest collection, however big the site or budget available, can't hope to collect everything available and a degree of selectivity must be applied. For example, there are over 600 species of oaks alone, and even a collection specialising in the genus won't be able to provide the space or range of climatic conditions to grow them all. For this reason, all collections have to decide on the scope of their intended plant acquisition. For some, this means specialisation, while others choose to take a more generalist approach, sacrificing depth in any area for breadth and diversity.

Deciding What To Collect

All collections are different, and the process of deciding what to collect will be influenced by a number of factors, some of which may provide an opportunity to be distinctive through specialisation of some sort.

Clearly, the most important consideration is the collection's objectives but there will be other factors that influence the choice of plants.

For most collections, there are more important considerations than simply trying to gather as many taxa as possible. In particular, it should be remembered that the choice of species not only sets the botanical basis of the collection but will also have a major influence on its physical landscape. A collection of conifers, for example, will inevitably create a very different landscape from one with a wider variety of tree and shrub types. (PLATE 34)

Since almost all collections have at least some aspiration of attaining garden status, an important aspect of plant selection must be the ornamental qualities of at least a proportion of the plants chosen. This is especially so for those collections reliant on public popularity for financial support through donation or paying visits. Only a proportion of visitors are likely to come purely for the scientific aspects of the garden; for the rest, it is the aesthetic qualities that will determine whether they visit again. This may mean that some species are repeated through the collection to provide continuity and landscape cohesion. Conversely, a collection created with a one-of-each approach may lack these qualities, however appealing it may be to botanical "twitchers"! The subject of landscape design is covered in more detail in Chapter 2.

As well as the number of different types (or taxa) of plants in a collection, there is also the question of overall number of individuals. One of the most common shortfalls of many tree collections, particularly in the early stages of their development, is a tendency to cram in as many rare and interesting plants as possible without considering the need for growing space.

Limitations on species choice

Before starting to decide what species to grow it may be useful to consider the limiting factors and the constraints they may impose. As well as the obvious restrictions of available area and budget, there are other factors associated with the site, location, or staffing:

▲ Climate. Rainfall, winter temperatures, and a number of other climatic factors will greatly limit the species that can be successfully grown. Species suitability in relation to cold tolerance may be judged by reference to the system of climate zones, but care should be taken since these provide only a crude guide to hardiness. Likewise, annual rainfall figures may provide only part of the story: is the rainfall unevenly distributed with long dry spells that may rule out some species? Rainfall may be supplemented by irrigation, but this could be expensive or go against the collection's environmental philosophy. Short of using green houses, the natural climatic limits can be extended to some extent by using hardier sheltering and shade plants.

Plant collectors have always tended to test the limits of hardiness by planting species at the edge of their climatic comfort zones. Predicted climate change may mean that climatic zones will shift at unprecedented rates in the next few decades, allowing formerly tender plants to thrive.

▲ Soil types and other site characteristics. These are discussed in more detail in the section on site selection in Chapter 2. Factors such as pH and drainage may have a major influence on possible species choice.

▲ Disease problems. Some diseases, such as fire blight caused by the bacterium *Erwinia amylovora*, may be particularly common in some areas, to the extent that susceptible species become unviable. Some species may provide the host for diseases of other plants and should be planted only after the risks are fully considered. For example, the pathogen that causes sudden oak death, *Phytophthora ramorum*, also infects rhododendrons and some other genera. To protect rare or valuable species susceptible to the disease, the precaution may be taken not to grow rhododendrons.

▲ Cultural requirements. Some plants have cultivation requirements that may be impossible or difficult to provide. Flowering shrubs that require frequent pruning may be a poor, unrealistic choice in an arboretum with insufficient staff to maintain them.

▲ Space. Where space is at a premium, large trees may be unsuitable.

▲ Invasiveness. Some species may be unsuitable for planting in certain countries or geographical areas due to their invasive qualities. European holly (*Ilex aquifolium*), for example, has become a problem species in the Pacific Northwest, where it spreads into indigenous forests. In some countries, government agencies produce lists of unsuitable or banned species, and contravention may result in prosecution. In the USA, the United States Department of Agriculture (USDA) gives advice through its online National Invasive Species Information Center.

▲ Dangerous plants. A few species may be considered unsuitable due to the risk to visitors. This may include poisonous-berried species or those with stems armed with thorns. The suitability of these species will depend on the level and type of public use, and it may be a question of limiting their planting to certain locations only.

Matching trees to objectives

Again, defining the range (or scope) of trees to be grown will depend directly on the collection's objectives. Some scientific collections take a tightly focussed approach and may limit their range of trees and shrubs to particular families, genera, or even individual species with little regard to popularity with the general public. For them the scoping process is a simple one. More horticulturally focussed collections may concentrate on shrubs suitable for particular garden situations. For others, and particularly those with a community or public role, the aim is likely to be to accession a wide range of plants to demonstrate the variability of the tree world as well as create an attractive treescape. In this case the result will be a blend of plants that matches the relative importance of these objectives.

In Chapter 2, the examination of mission statements demonstrated the typical range of objectives for various arboretums. From this can be generated a list of the categories of tree and shrub species required based on the objectives identified. The following are the most common categories:

▲ Botanical or horticultural objectives. Plants that give the collection its interest as a botanical collection. These may be a speciality group of plants or even form a national collection.

▲ Scientific objectives. Plants that support any research being carried out. This may be taxonomic research related to a particular group of plants or practical investigation into the effects of climate or horticultural techniques. A phenology trial of species to monitor the rate of climate change is an example.

▲ Conservation objectives. Plants that are the subjects of conservation efforts. In most circumstances, these will be ex situ trees, perhaps collected from the wild with the specific intention of preserving an endangered species. For some species, plants in cultivation represent a significant part (or even the entirety) of the world's population. Even where plants cannot be said to contribute to conservation efforts directly, they may provide opportunity for interpretation and learning about issues of conservation. (PLATE 35)

▲ Educational objectives. Plants that support specific or wider learning objectives of the collection. Some well-developed collections with a public function often have learning or educational strategies, and these are the plants that will support the themes and programs identified. This subject is dealt with in more detail in the section on interpretation in Chapter 6.

▲ Aesthetic requirements. Almost all collections have, at least as a minor objective, the desire to look good and, for many, the need to attract paying visitors makes this an essential element of plant choice. But an attractive landscape needs more than just accent plants. Brightly coloured or unusual plants require less flamboyant complementary ones to provide continuity or structure. Evergreen species often serve this purpose and may, as a secondary function, give shade or shelter.

▲ Cultural or historical requirements. Many existing collections have a distinctive range of trees that sets them apart from others. The species represented may be from a particular historical era or contribute to a design style associated with the site.

▲ Shelter/shade or other functional requirements. Many collections try to push the climatic limits imposed by their local environment and grow plants more suited to warmer or more sheltered conditions. This may be achieved by using more hardy species to shade or shelter important botanical specimens. These "supporting actors" may be grown with little consideration for appearance, or be an intrinsic part of the collection with an aesthetic as well as a practical function. Native trees well adapted to local conditions are often the best candidates, but carefully selected exotics may double-up as collection specimens in their own right.

Of course in practice, these functions overlap greatly, and many plants serve a number of purposes. The proportions of plants from each group will depend on the arboretum's unique character and objectives, but most collections will include plants from at least three or four of them.

Layout and types of collections

The subject of plant arrangement in relation to landscape design was dealt with in Chapter 2. But as well as the question of aesthetic layout, it is important to consider the various functional options for arranging the collection. Some collections incorporate plants of all kinds and functions into one unitary landscape. Others are broken into specialist sub-collections, each with their own characteristics, objectives, and contribution to the overall wider collection. Many collections choose to combine elements of both by incorporating specialist elements within a more generalist collection. These various layouts may have been planned and represented spatially in the master plan. Of course, there's no reason why a specialist sub-collection can't be mixed throughout a wider collection for best landscape effect. A collection of holly cultivars, for example, needn't be put all in one place but may be spread among other genera for best complementary effect. One of the great advantages of modern database and mapping systems is their ability to generate maps and lists of selected groups of plants. This allows students or other people wishing to study a particular plant group an easy way to find them all even in a dispersed collection like this.

Despite the range of possible arrangements and degrees of specialisation, it is possible to describe various distinct collection types. The most common ones are the following:

- ▲ Representative collections. This is one of the most common kinds of collection and one that is suited to general collections where the intention is to display trees and shrubs from a broad range of families. It is a good model for many small public arboretums established to provide a range of educational and interpretive opportunities; it results in an interesting and diverse landscape as well.
- ▲ Specialist collections. The most common type of specialisation is to limit the plants grown to a particular family, genus, or other botanical group. Collections of this kind are sometimes described as systematic since they rely on the system of taxonomic classification. This is a common model in collections established with scientific or educational objectives. Some arboretums also develop collections of cultivar groups to display the range of options for private gardeners. The Brooklyn Botanic Garden in New York, for example, has a collection of crape myrtles for this purpose as well as to provide a dazzling display.

  Some of these types of collection may be registered with wider organisations. The North American Plant Collections Consortium (NAPCC) is a network of participating botanical collections with specialist collections of this kind, including ones based on family, genus, and cultivars. In the UK many arboretums and botanic gardens contribute to the National Plant Collection Scheme, administered by Plant Heritage (formerly the National Council for the Conservation of Plants and Gardens), which exists to help conserve plants of wild and cultivated origin. (PLATE 36)
- ▲ Thematic collections. Many arboretums choose to develop themes that may cut across taxonomic groups. These themes are often derived from learning objectives. They may be geographical (trees of a particular area), ethnobotanical (trees used by people), historical (trees originally planted in the garden), or any number of other themes. Of course, there is considerable scope for overlap between systematic and thematic types—a collection of attractively barked maples, for example, combines both systematic (maples) and the-

matic (ornamental bark) elements. Thematic elements like these will be derived from the arboretum's objectives and be developed through various programs of activity. (PLATE 37)

▲ Conservation collections. These are collections established to contribute to the conservation of rare or endangered species. The most valuable collections of this kind include a number of individuals from each taxon to provide representation of at least some of its genetic variability. Many collections derive their direction from wider national or international conservation objectives, such as the Global Strategy for Plant Conservation. The strategy is in turn derived from the Convention on Biological Diversity and provides sixteen targets for practical action. These targets include a number relevant to collectors of all plants, including trees and shrubs. As well as establishing ex situ collections of rare or endangered species, arboretums may contribute to conservation through management of native habitat or education and interpretive programs to raise awareness of the issues involved.

Accession plans

An accession plan is a written document to help managers make objective decisions about the plants to be included in the collection. It provides a summary of considerations, such as site limitations, intended collection types, landscape requirements, and other matters dealt with earlier in the chapter. As plants are considered for accessioning, it is the standard to test their suitability against the collection's objectives. This document often forms part of an overall collection policy (see Chapter 2) and is one of the most important sources of reference for any arboretum. The plan needn't be complicated or lengthy but should be sufficiently specific to guide current and future managers. There are various ways that these plans can be written to do this.

For small arboretums with relatively few trees and shrubs, it may be possible to draw up a list of all the species wanted along with the number of each. These plants can then be acquired from a suitable source and planted in the places decided for them. But for larger collections a more flexible approach is required to allow for the uncertainties of plant acquisition and the dynamic nature of any garden or plant collection. The Campus Arboretum of the University of Arizona, USA, draws directly from its objectives to provide a list of criteria into which plant accessions should fit:

▲ educational/interpretive or research potential
▲ functional or landscape potential
▲ preservation of rare cultivated plants, especially those which honor the University's heritage
▲ dominance or importance within a pertinent eco-geographic region
▲ economic or ethnobotanic utility
▲ ex situ conservation of taxa

This model is one that can easily be adapted to meet the general needs of a municipal or local community arboretum established in an existing park. A simple statement for such a collection may say, "The arboretum will grow tree species and cultivars in order to—

▲ display examples of a diverse range of hardy trees and shrubs to represent the common genera grown in the area;
▲ provide opportunities for themed trails for recreational and educational purposes;
▲ provide year-round ornamental interest;
▲ maintain the park's 'sense of place' based on the tree heritage established since its creation in the 19th century."

From these guidelines and requirements, the suitability of plants, including those offered by donors, can be judged against objective criteria. Groups establishing collections of this kind may also seek advice from a variety of sources. Some local government planning departments provide lists of suitable trees for planting schemes, while many books include a selector that arranges species according to their size, cultural requirements, and ornamental attributes.

Another, more detailed approach to crafting an accession plan is based on a list of genera with a brief description on each. This may also introduce an element of prioritisation, as shown in Table 1.

TABLE 1. FRAGMENT OF AN ACCESSION PLAN.

GENUS	PRIORITY	STATEMENT
Acer	1	National collection, all hardy taxa
Carya	3	Native species only
Magnolia	4	Ornamental species for spring interest
Quercus	2	Representatives from all temperate regions

Key to codes:
1 = priority (national and core collections, conservation status, or other high priority taxa)
2 = high (important components of general representative collection)
3 = medium (less important components of general representative collection)
4 = low (include only for ornamental or other landscape qualities)

Removing plants—de-accessioning

Trees may have to be removed for a variety of reasons. In order to guard against the risk of unintentional loss of valuable plants, particularly those of conservation status, a check procedure should be followed. This is rather like the reverse of that used to accession plants. Each time removal of a plant is considered, managers should check its value and whether it is the only representative of a particular species or accession. Where the plant is considered valuable or irreplaceable, cuttings or other propagules may be taken to ensure the genetic material is conserved.

Existing trees and old collections

Many collections develop on a site with existing trees, perhaps planted in a particular style. In this case, decisions will have to be made at an early stage: do these trees contribute to the intended collection, or can they, at least, be incorporated into it to provide early shelter or landscape structure? In some cases the established trees and their style of layout may actually provide the initial direction from which the species list is developed. This is often the case where historical collections are being rejuvenated or new collections established on a site with trees associated with its previous history. As well as the potential benefits of retaining existing trees, it should be remembered that each one kept will limit the space for planting of new trees that may contribute more to the collection's objectives. The decision of whether or not to retain these trees and incorporate them into the collection should use the accession plan as the source of reference.

Species choice and climate change

Plant collectors all over the world increasingly need to consider the possible effects of projected global climate change. Predicting the likely changes in the various aspects of climate cannot be done with certainty, but most scientists agree on general trends, if not precise detail. The knock-on effects on trees and shrubs adds another level of uncertainty, but it is almost certain that changing patterns of rainfall and seasonal temperatures will test the resilience of many plants, particularly those on the margins of their natural climatic limits. Added to this is the likelihood that pest and diseases will migrate with climate changes or become more pathogenic.

Attempting to preempt these changes by adapting the range of species grown is a difficult task. Complex interactions between different aspects of climate and plants are hard to predict. However, collectors should begin to think about steps they can take to make their tree populations more resilient. In particular, they should take the following actions:

▲ Test new species, including geographic or cultivated varieties. A proportion of these are likely to fail, but this will help to inform future planting.
▲ Improve the matching of plant to site. This may be done by analysis of the soil properties and temperature patterns in the arboretum so that plants can be better matched to the most suitable locations.
▲ Avoid overdependence on a few species, particularly those known to

be drought intolerant or prone to disease. It is also important to consider the age range of valuable species—old trees may be more vulnerable, and a program of gradual replacement may be necessary.
▲ Cooperate with other collections to establish backup collections of
vulnerable plants.
▲ Record disease prevalence or other reasons for failure to help inform future accession plans.

Acquisition

Closely linked to the subject of accession is that of acquisition: the
sources and mechanisms by which plants are obtained. The two terms—
accession and acquisition—are intimately related, and the distinction
between them varies between plant collections. For most collections,
obtaining plants is a relatively straightforward matter of purchase from
nurseries or acceptance of gifts from supporters. But for institutional
collections with a need to acquire rare or wild-origin plants, clear policies covering international regulations on plant movement, ethical considerations, and plant hygiene safeguards must be in place. Together,
policies and plans on accession and acquisition provide the guidance
required to ensure the right trees are added to the collection, and they
are obtained in ways that conform to the ethics and environmental
standards laid down in the mission and objectives for the collection.

There are various ways by which collectors can go about obtaining
the plants from the lists or criteria defined in the accession plan. Choice
of the most appropriate will depend on the nature of the collection, its
objectives, and the particular plants being sought. Broadly speaking,
these various plant sources may be divided into commercial and non-
commercial types.

Obtaining Plants—Commercial Sources

On the surface, the question of where and how to acquire plants may
seem an easy one to answer. Most people wanting to buy trees or shrubs

for a garden simply find a local nursery or garden centre that stocks the plants they want and go and buy them. And even for collectors with a longer shopping list and very specific needs, this is often a perfectly suitable approach to take. Commercial growers vary greatly from impersonal chain stores to small family-owned nurseries run by enthusiasts who combine business with pleasure. Both kinds of establishments can play their part in sourcing trees, but for most collectors, the personal service and knowledge to be found in the latter makes them a more rewarding and fruitful source of plants. Some collectors build up a relationship with suppliers, who may go out of their way to source or even propagate plants for them. In this way, growers may be introduced to species or cultivars they had not previously known and use their relationship with a knowledgeable collector to add new plants to their commercial lists. More specialist growers produce and distribute regularly updated catalogues and provide a mail-order service to customers spread over a wide geographical range. The rise of the Internet has further increased the ability of collectors and suppliers to communicate, and made it economic to produce and trade an ever-growing range of "minority" plant species. Seeking the tree you want can be as simple as entering a plant name into a search engine and selecting from the range of suppliers listed. In the UK, the Royal Horticultural Society (RHS) publishes a well-known Plant Finder updated annually. This list of plants and the growers who can supply them is now available online (see "Links to Tree Organisations and Networks"). Plant suppliers' Web sites have become informative and attractive, with catalogues of available plants supplemented with photographs and a range of useful facts about the growth requirements and attributes of the species on offer. Ordering is usually quick and easy, and improved packaging and transportation means that young trees generally arrive at their destination in good condition. The only major downside of this method of acquisition is the inability to examine the plants before purchase. But good suppliers rely on their reputation for quality and build a loyal following with customers who are happy to recommend them to other collectors. (PLATE 38)

Plant selection

Unless plants are being purchased blind from mail-order sources, some level of selection is possible and can be an important means of ensuring that the best plants are obtained. This is a large subject, and studious readers are advised to seek detailed advice from a more specialist publication, including those in the reading list at the back of this book. The following are some general guidance points.

Health and vigour. Most modern nurseries and plant centres provide plants of a consistently good quality. However, it is worth looking carefully for signs of poor health. Diseased or low-vigour plants should be rejected, however desirable they may be for their rarity or other qualities. Most problems are easily spotted even by inexperienced buyers and include small or discoloured leaves, signs of pests or pest damage, poor growth, or damaged bark on stems or branches. In addition, container-grown plants should be examined for root constriction resulting from plants spending too long in an undersized pot.

Bare-rooted and container-grown plants. Bare-rooted plants are grown in the open ground before being dug up shortly before sale. They are more common in commercial forestry or horticulture than ornamental or amenity trees. Great care in handling is required if damage or desiccation of delicate roots is to be avoided.

Most plants sold by domestic plant suppliers are container-grown, and this type of plant is the best bet for most collectors. The great advantage is the ability to transplant from container to soil without disturbance to the roots. This makes it possible to plant trees at any time of year, provided they are watered during dry spells. The only potential disadvantage is a reluctance in some plants for their roots to spread and develop beyond the comfort of their pot compost once planted in the open ground.

Size. Choice of size is a trade-off between immediate impact, cost, and the greater likelihood large plants have to suffer a marked slowdown in growth, or "check," when transplanted. The optimum balance of these factors will vary from one situation to another, but as a general rule it is best to use plants just large enough to have sufficient reserves to survive their new environment. This is usually best judged by their stem diameter rather than height. Some species, such as hickories and tupelos, are known for their reluctance to transplant successfully unless the operation is carried out when the trees are very young. Where large standard plants are wanted, those with large root balls in relation to their crowns should be selected.

Labels and naming. Collectors shouldn't assume that plant labels will always be accurate. This is particularly true of non-specialist suppliers selling unusual or rare plants. As well as incorrect labelling, horticultural nomenclature often varies from that used by botanists. Where doubt exists, plant identification should be verified by a knowledgeable botanist.

Obtaining Plants—Non-commercial Sources

However good many plant centres and commercial growers are these days, there are still circumstances where other methods of plant acquisition are preferable. This is particularly true for the more ambitious tree collector, and especially one whose accession policy places an emphasis on plants rarely seen in cultivation, or of known origin. Off-the-shelf purchase may also lack the element of excitement often sought by collectors of all kinds—though the chance find of an interesting plant in a garden centre can still provide a thrill of discovery! Many collectors also derive satisfaction from an involvement in the propagation and raising of young trees, particularly where this involves collecting seed or cuttings from well-known or favourite plants.

Donations and swaps

Donation or swapping of plants from one collector to another forms an important part of the culture of tree collecting as it does in other fields, and some small public collections rely almost entirely on donated plants for their development. But collectors being offered plants by well-meaning donors should be wary of always accepting for fear of giving offence by declining the offer. These donated plants may come from a variety of sources or methods of propagation, and questions of verification, ethics, plant hygiene, and contribution to the accession plan should all be considered. On the more positive side, donations from other collectors may provide an opportunity to obtain otherwise unobtainable species, varieties, or individual plants. For collections involved in conserving rare species, passing some plants to other collectors may also provide a backup against disease or other catastrophic loss. Small collections may benefit from developing relationships with larger institutional ones. Despite their size, even the largest collections rarely have all the space (or sometimes the soil types) they would like. In exchange for growing space, smaller collectors may get trees as well as advice from these sources.

Owners of champion trees or individual plants with unique historical or horticultural significance may agree to propagate and donate plants if requested. The offspring of these trees may be no different from others with less distinguished credentials, but they provide a range of opportunities for interpretation and storytelling. In the UK, the Millennium was commemorated by a program of propagating yew trees from many of the oldest trees known. Offspring were distributed to collectors all over the country to provide inspiration for interpretation about the heritage of these yew trees and their longevity.

Index semina and surplus lists

Many scientific institutions, particularly universities and larger botanical gardens, produce lists of surplus seed. These index semina are sent to plant collectors, who may apply for and obtain seed from these lists. In addition, some collections, and particularly those with their own propagation facilities, produce and distribute surplus plant lists to other collectors. Providing the donors' conditions can be met, both these sources can be valuable means by which even small private collectors can obtain plants.

Propagation from existing collection trees

Propagation is the term used to describe the range of horticultural techniques used to grow new plants from existing ones. Having the ability to propagate new plants from those already in the collection has a number of possible advantages. The main ones are described in Table 2 (pages 85 and 86). On the other hand, investing in the staff and facilities required to undertake more than occasional or small-scale propagation may be beyond the scope of most collectors. Even a simple frost-free glasshouse with an irrigation system and benches for cuttings and seed trays is expensive to buy and run. (PLATE 39)

In nature, the most common way by which plants propagate themselves is by seed arising from sexual reproduction, usually with different plants providing the male and female gametes. The individual progeny are each unique genetic intermediates of their parents, often showing subtle variations in appearance, one from another. This variety is the cutting edge by which natural selection shapes evolution and allows species to adapt to change. It is also the essential element that allows plant breeders to select and accentuate desirable attributes and create cultivars. In order to replicate them without further variation, growers have developed various vegetative methods of propagation that utilise parts of the plant other than seed. This also allows them to produce identical and numerous copies of the plants they want. These vegetative techniques utilise the ability of plants to reproduce by non-sexual methods. In the wild, many species demonstrate this ability and, for some, this mode has become the norm, with sexual reproduction occurring only occasionally if at all. An example of this can be seen in some kinds of elms in Europe, where suckering from roots has become the method by which trees spread widely along hedges and into fields. Other species have the ability to reproduce by layering, where a low branch comes into contact with the soil and produces roots and ultimately an independent new plant. Some, like certain species of *Sorbus*, produce fertile seed asexually without the need for pollination. Unlike those arising from sexual reproduction, the progeny of these asexual methods are identical copies, or clones, of the parent plant. Of course the resulting uniformity eliminates the potential for natural or artificial selection but has the alternative advantage of eliminating the uncertainty and wastefulness associated with sexual means. In the artificial environment of a garden, the close proximity of related plants from all over the world greatly increases the chance of hybridisation. Although this may bring about fortuitous hybrids that turn out to be of horticultural value, it has the downside of making it difficult to preserve the genetic integrity of the original plant. Oaks, for example, are renowned for their "promiscuity," so that acorns grown from trees in a collection of different species will very likely give rise to hybrid plants of uncertain parentage. This is another area where vegetative propagation is a valuable tool, since it eliminates the possibility of producing unwanted hybrids. (PLATE 40)

Vegetative propagation is a large and specialised subject too big for this book, but it is useful to be aware of the main methods used and their advantages. By far the most common techniques adopted for propagating trees are stem cutting and grafting. The former relies on the ability of a cut stem to produce its own roots. Some groups of plants, notably willows and poplars, do this very readily without the need for special care or treatment. Others require more skill and attention and even the use of specialist equipment or hormones. The time during the growing season at which the cuttings are taken is also an important factor determining the successful rooting of cuttings, with different plant groups having different requirements. (PLATE 41)

Collection from the wild

All garden plants originate from wild ancestors, and plant collecting started with people gathering plants from the wild. Most of our modern gardens owe much to the activity of plant collectors, who for hundreds of years have searched the world for new and exciting species. But why, now that there are so many plants already in cultivation, should we need to continue to collect from the wild? This is an important question, particularly since human activity is posing a threat to so many of the forested habitats of the world. This last sentence provides both a warning and also a possible justification for wild collecting. On the one hand, wild collection provides a means of obtaining plants of known origin as genetic representatives of the world's habitats and geographical regions. As described earlier, these may form part of an ex situ reserve for conservation or a valuable scientific resource for study of a species and its variability. On the other hand, it is vital in the modern era, that collecting is carried out in an environmentally sustainable and morally sound way. But wild collection should not necessarily be regarded as essential or even desirable. For many collections, the objectives will not include ex situ conservation or even detailed species-level study, and plants derived from existing garden sources may be just as good. On the other hand, studying trees in the wild (even if not collected) can provide staff with an insight into their true nature and stimulate interest and greater knowledge.

Collecting plants in the wild needn't involve expeditions to other countries, and the potential for collecting plants from local natural sources should not be overlooked. Many collections are established to display native species, and their collection and cultivation can be a valuable means of involving community or school groups in this fascinating area of work. Seed-collecting expeditions to local hedgerows and woods are events in themselves that can provide opportunities to learn about these natural habitats as well as propagation of the species found in them.

Where it is decided that wild collection can contribute to the collection objectives, it is important to produce a rationale to ensure that those taking part in the venture as well as sponsors and hosts are clear about the objectives and how they will be met. Once prepared, this rationale will also help those involved in the trip prepare thoroughly. Time spent at this stage will pay dividends later by avoiding wasted time and effort once the expedition is underway. Lists of target species for each expedition should be drawn up and detailed itineraries with collecting sites prepared. It is also important for those collecting to spend time sharpening their knowledge of the plants to be sought. Most collectors work with institutions or individuals in the country to be visited. University departments, government forestry agencies, or corresponding arboretums may all provide support through information on suitable sites, accommodation, or help with obtaining permits to collect. The help of a local botanist is a major advantage on collecting expeditions, for their detailed knowledge of both indigenous plants and botanical names. (PLATE 42)

The ethics of plant collecting. Historically, plant collectors have often given little thought to the well-being of the plant or human populations in the areas from which they have collected. Forests were seen as a limitless resource to be exploited for their plant treasure. In the modern, more socially enlightened and environmentally aware era, consideration must be given to the sustainability and equitable sharing of the benefits of plant collecting. As well as personal responsibility, international conventions to control and regulate the collection and transfer of plant material have been agreed to. The most important of these are the Convention on Biological Diversity (CBD) and the Convention on International Trade in Endangered Species (CITES). The former is a treaty to sustain the diversity of life on earth and promote equitable sharing of the benefits arising from it; it came into force in 1993 and has been ratified by over 180 nations. CITES is a more specific convention that provides regularly updated lists of threatened species and sets clear rules for their trade. These documents and others derived from them should be fully complied with by all those collecting and importing plants from wild sources. In particular, collectors should always ensure that they have permission to collect (with written permits) from the land owner or relevant government agency.

Selection of the collecting area and timing. Most collectors, unless they are very familiar with the country in which they are collecting, take advice from local experts. These people will also be able to give advice on the best times to collect based on seed ripening.

The choice of possible sites is often limited by logistical problems such as transport or time available. In many countries, collection permits may be difficult to obtain, particularly for national parks or other conservation areas. For these reasons, the range of possible sites may be very restricted. But where there is choice, sites should be chosen according to various factors, including the following:

▲ Botanical suitability/diversity. Does the site contain the plants on the target list? Collection itineraries may be planned to obtain the greatest number of accessions from the least possible sites to maximise the use of time, or concentrate on sites with the most sought-after species.

▲ Naturalness/lack of disturbance. It may be tempting to collect from easily accessible areas close to cities but, since the main aim is to obtain plants of wild and natural origin, it is important to avoid areas significantly altered by human cultivation and other activity.

▲ Altitude. Wild plants are adapted to their local climatic conditions. Many of the trees and shrubs grown in collections originate in areas of much higher or lower latitude from that of their resident country. Collecting at high (or lower) altitude can greatly influence the hardiness of the plants accessioned by "correcting" for this difference.

▲ Ease of access. This includes both access to the site and movement within it once there.

Seed collecting. By far the most common method of plant collecting is by seed. Not only is seed far easier to handle and transport than other kinds of plant material, but it is generally considered to pose a lower risk of transferring pathogens. In order to maximise the value of the seed collected, it is important to follow a methodology. (PLATE 43)

▲ Select parent plants. It is best to collect from a number of plants spread over the collecting area in order to obtain a variety of genetic material.

▲ Examine the seed being collected, and reject poorly formed or overripe seed. A hand lens is useful for this purpose.

▲ Collect more seed than is required to allow for poor germination, or provide a surplus for donating to other collectors or, where appropriate, seed banks.

▲ Record the seed being collected as you go along, and label clearly to avoid later confusion.

Seed handling. Nothing is more disappointing than arriving home from a well-planned collecting expedition to find that the valuable seed, carefully gathered and recorded, has turned into a mushy and useless mess in the bags. All newly collected seed should be checked for pests or disease. Dry seed may need little more than an occasional inspection to check that it hasn't gone mouldy, but moist seed and especially those contained in a berry or other wet fruit will require additional work.

Busy days in the field may be followed by late nights back at camp or hotel carrying out seed cleaning or sorting. The choice of bags is an important consideration to help keep seed at a suitable humidity. Some kinds of seed (known as recalcitrant seed) should not be allowed to dry too much, while others need to be kept open to avoid mould formation or even decomposition. A mix of paper and plastic bags along with absorbent tissue may be used to get the best level of drying. (PLATES 44 AND 45)

Recording seed collection. Having said that the main justification for undertaking seed collection in the wild is to accession plants of known origin, it is vital that accurate records be kept. Of these, by far the most important are location and altitude. The former may be descriptive but should also include grid reference derived either from a map or handheld GPS. The level and detail of other information recorded depends on the purpose for which the plants are being collected. Table 3 shows other important information that should be recorded and a simple form for recording it, either as a paper template or computer spreadsheet. It is especially important to allocate a unique collection number at the time of collection. This may be a new accession number in line with the garden's cataloguing system (see Chapter 5) but will more likely be an expedition number that is converted to an accession number once home. Plant names should be as complete as possible, but plants should not be rejected just because they cannot be fully identified. They may, on later verification, be found to be of great value. See Table 3 on page 87.

Herbarium and voucher samples. Collectors on expeditions often collect samples of leaves, shoots, flowers, or other plant material in addition to seeds. These may later be used to confirm identification of the plants from which seed is collected or donated to herbaria to contribute to their permanent plant inventory. The former, often referred to as voucher samples, may be essential for ensuring that the full scientific value of the plants collected can be realised. They may be kept as a short-term source of reference or incorporated into a wider herbarium collection once they have fulfilled their initial function. (PLATE 46)

Collecting and preserving herbarium samples is a job that requires skill and attention to detail, as well as various materials and equipment.

Plant presses and layers of paper for drying can be heavy and unwieldy and add an additional challenge to collectors, particularly in difficult terrain. For this reason, some people choose to use digital photography as a quicker and less arduous alternative to actual plant material. This should, however, be regarded as a "second best" option.

Those seeking more advice on collecting herbarium samples should refer to a more specialised publication or Web site.

Equipment. The amount and variety of equipment needed for a plant-collecting expedition depends on factors such as the location, whether or not herbarium samples are being collected, and the type of seed or plant material being sought. But the following is a list of equipment that will be required on most trips:

- collection bags of various sizes and materials (waterproof or breathable), with ties and tags
- secateurs, pruning saw, knife, long-reach loppers, hand lens
- plant presses and absorbent paper for drying wet seed and plant material
- ropes, harnesses, and other climbing equipment, if climbing is required
- collection book or PC
- navigation/location equipment—GPS, compass, altimeter
- pens and pencils
- photographic equipment—camera, tripod, macro lens
- binoculars (useful to spot seed from the ground)
- first aid kit

When put together, this can be quite a daunting load, which is why most expeditions take a number of participants to contribute to the carrying, seed cleaning, recording, and other jobs.

TABLE 2. PLANT SOURCES.

SOURCE	ADVANTAGES	DISADVANTAGES
Purchase from a commercial plant centre or nursery	Simple and, where small numbers of plants are involved, cheap. Ability to specify what, when, and number of plants. Can choose supplier based on price and quality. No need for propagation staff or facilities.	Supply of unusual species may be problematic. Expensive for large numbers of plants. May be a potential for disease introduction. Horticultural naming often conflicts with or lags behind that used by botanists and plant collectors, leading to confusion.
Mail order and e-sales from commercial sources	Allows easy access to specialist nurseries and other suppliers and therefore a very wide range of plants.	Plant quality may be unpredictable. Remote selection prevents direct contact with plants.
Gifts from other plant collectors, surplus lists, index semina, plant networks, etc.	May be a source of rare plants and those of known provenance and origin. Can be a way of cementing relationships with other collections.	Unless reciprocal favours can be given, may lead to feeling of unequal favour. May have to "take or leave" what is available—no control of timing or quality.
Propagation from existing trees in the collection (assumes that propagation is carried out by direct staff; some collections contract independent propagators to carry out such work for them)	Allows propagation of locally well-known, historically significant, or rare trees. May be cheap—where large numbers of trees are produced. Reduces risk of import of disease—particularly for some prone genera. Provides an opportunity for skills training and active involvement by volunteers.	Requires skilled staff and propagation facilities. Plants take at least two or three years from propagation to planting.

TABLE 2. PLANT SOURCES (continued).

SOURCE	ADVANTAGES	DISADVANTAGES
Collection expeditions from wild plants	Allows the opportunity to acquire plants not in cultivation, unavailable commercially, and of known and recorded origin. Provides opportunities for staff to participate in plant collecting expeditions. Provides opportunities to cooperate with other collections to share costs and skills and develop partnerships.	Expensive. Requires collection permits, plant passports, and other time-consuming administration and paperwork.
Direct collection from other collections	Allows propagation from known and possibly very unusual plants. Helps to build relationships with other collectors.	Requires permission. Takes time and probably travel. Requires staff and facilities to propagate the plants collected.

TABLE 3. COLLECTION RECORDING FORM.

Date:
Country:
Location:
Collectors:

COLLECTION NUMBER	TAXON	LATITUDE	LONGITUDE	ALTITUDE	NO. OF PLANTS COLLECTED FROM	ACCOMPANYING PLANTS	NOTES

4 ▲ Caring for the Trees
Maintenance and Management

F
or most tree enthusiasts who have the opportunity to plant or manage a tree collection, it is the process of gathering and planting that
holds the main appeal. In the rush of enthusiasm, some collectors
may not think far beyond the initial preparation of the site and the
planting of trees. However, nothing stands still in the arboretum, just as
in any other garden, and a program of active management will be necessary to maintain what's already there and move the collection toward
its ultimate objectives. At the most basic level, this means the constant
cycle of planting, maintenance, and removal of dead or unwanted plants
that is the lifeblood of any garden. But even the most modest collection
will be situated in a landscape containing a number of other features
and kinds of vegetation that require maintenance. These may be artificial or natural, but their presence and condition will have an impact on
the tree collection and its function, both positive and potentially nega-
tive. In large institutional arboretums, these non-collection features
may become extensive and highly developed, requiring specialist staff
and equipment to maintain them. So the maintenance of an arboretum,
like any garden, requires a combination of tools, equipment, and materials, managed by people with relevant skills and dedication. (PLATE 47)

This chapter aims to provide advice on the maintenance and management of a tree collection once it is past the stage of initial planting.
The two terms are closely related, but here management is the broad
term used to describe the development and implementation of a planned
program of practical work aimed at meeting the objectives of the collection. Maintenance refers to day-to-day practices used to keep things
running and looking as they should. The chapter starts by considering

why and how much maintenance is needed, and its planning and organisation, before considering the techniques and skills needed to carry it out.

Maintenance—Why and How Much?

No two gardens or arboretums are quite alike, and the requirement for their maintenance varies greatly. By the nature of the plants they contain, tree collections can generally be maintained less intensively and with fewer personnel than a similar sized garden of herbaceous plants. Once established, trees can, if desired, be left largely to their own devices, requiring only occasional inspection and essential pruning. Indeed, in woodland gardens the aim may be to capture the unkempt atmosphere of a natural forest, albeit in a cultivated form free from the discomfort and inconveniences of the real thing! But for most arboretums and tree collections, even those dedicated mainly to science rather than ornament, some level of maintenance of the plants and landscape will be necessary. The extent and nature of this will depend on the objectives and a whole range of other factors, including the kinds of trees and shrubs to be grown and the anticipated level of public usage. The latter is particularly true where paying visitors are an important source of income. Visitors, even hardened tree enthusiasts, want to see plants maintained in a visually attractive way, and for the less dedicated stroller, quality of paths and other artificial facilities may be almost as important as the trees themselves. So how do you decide what maintenance is required?

Since most arboretums have a limited budget and number of staff, the more relevant question is usually how much maintenance can we afford and where are the priorities? Consideration of the likely maintenance budget should be part of the planning of any collection in order to avoid unrealistic expectations. This is partly down to limiting the size of the collection to what can be looked after, a discipline that is often overlooked by enthusiastic planters! Another consideration is to decide what level of tending is desirable or appropriate to create the desired landscape quality. It is quite possible to over-maintain the trees and other elements of a garden landscape, resulting in a loss of its naturalistic atmosphere. Where appropriate, a lower level of maintenance may be adopted to create informality. This decision may be guided by a preexisting landscape style (for example, in an historic park) or may be arrived at for more pragmatic reasons of resource availability. In any case, when determining the maintenance needed it is often useful to consider work in terms of its level of importance—is it essential or just desirable? This may be helped by considering the reason for doing the various maintenance tasks being considered and where these fit into a hierarchy of priority. (PLATE 48)

The most common reasons for carrying out maintenance include the following:

▲ the safety of staff and visitors—"duty of care"
▲ other work required by law—management of protected species, conservation areas, etc.
▲ to maintain the health and value of the collection's trees and shrubs
▲ commercial reasons—to enhance income
▲ to maintain aesthetic quality
▲ expansion and development work

This list also places things in the likely order of priority, though that may vary to some extent depending on local circumstances. For example, short-term commercial considerations may be promoted in importance where they become vital to the continuation of the collection. Some types of work will also fulfil a number of objectives; as well as improving their aesthetic quality, pruning flowering shrubs is likely to make a collection more attractive to paying visitors and thereby boost income. Producing a list like this may help to identify maintenance jobs that are taking a disproportionate time to their value or others that need to be given greater priority. Intensive grass cutting may have begun at a time when there was a surplus of labour or on the whim of an individual with a love of well-kept lawns. But situations change, and a review of maintenance may lead to the conclusion that far less frequent cutting may be just as good and allow more time to be allocated to more valuable tasks. Very few gardens have as many staff members or other resources as they would like, and inevitably choices like this have to be made.

Determining maintenance requirements is a hard enough task for newly planted collections, but where a collection is being developed from existing mature trees, or the task is one of restoration of an established arboretum, it may be even more difficult to judge the level of labour and resources required. Much may depend on how many large trees have to be removed in the restorative phase and over what period of time this is carried out.

Visitor safety and the duty of care

It is a generally accepted legal principle in most countries that the owner or manager of an area of land owes a "duty of care" to people entering onto it, including members of staff. This is particularly relevant where people are being actively invited or charged for entry. This duty of care generally requires owners or managers to take necessary action to ensure the safety of visitors. It may take many forms, but of particular relevance to this chapter is the maintenance of features that could pose a significant hazard. This could be anything from a potholed path to a rotten branch over a path, but these safety-related jobs must be given priority. Regular inspections and keeping of records of remedial work is the basis for the safety management for all kinds of features; but, since this is a book about trees, it is the safety issues relating to trees and their maintenance that will be dealt with in more detail later in the chapter. (PLATE 49)

Landscape continuity and managing change

The long life span of most trees may give the impression of immortality, but disease, storms, and other extreme weather events will all take their toll on any population, sometimes at an alarming rate. As fears grow about the likelihood and possible consequences of global climate change, these concerns become even more acute along with the need to consider measures to ensure resilience and adaptability to change. There is no better insurance policy against these events than maintaining a balanced age structure with continual recruitment of young, vigorous trees and shrubs to take over when older ones are lost. But most tree collections start with a period of intensive planting of the space available, and the inevitable result is a more or less even-aged population, rather like that of a forest plantation—albeit with a wider range of species. Assuming that the aim is for some level of landscape continuity, this is a vulnerable position for a collection to find itself in. This may not be an important concern in the early years after establishment, but eventually the need for new planting will require difficult decisions to be made on the removal of less valuable or poor specimens to make room. This is a scenario familiar to managers inheriting mature or moribund collections where old trees dominate the landscape, leaving little or no space for planting their eventual replacements. In these situations there is no alternative to a proactive program of replacement, however unpopular and difficult this may be to "sell" to user groups. This, and other situations where additional or different kinds of resource and labour are needed, requires a special approach and possibly staff and equipment not used for general maintenance. Many collections regard significant changes like these as projects and manage them as such, with staff dedicated to the planning and fundraising required.

Organisation

As in any activity, planning and organisation of effort is the best way to make best use of the resources available and avoid unnecessary waste. At its simplest, this may be a purely instinctive process by a lone individual. But for larger and more complex collections where a number of people are engaged in a variety of tasks, plans also fulfil a function of coordinating effort and setting and maintaining standards. These plans may take various forms, but they are likely to be written documents produced with a clear idea of who they are intended to be read by.

Maintenance plans

Maintenance plans should identify the work to be carried out and have a time element to help ensure that all important maintenance is carried out at a suitable time and not overlooked. Inevitably, the production of maintenance plans will involve consideration of priorities, and it may be useful to classify jobs accordingly.

Many arboretums and gardens in general use a graded system of plans and schedules. The former may be spatial in nature, defining the maintenance requirement for each landscape type or area of the arboretum. The latter schedules will put a time scale or annual timetable to this work as a way of planning day-to-day allocation of staff and resource and as a way of monitoring progress.

These plans may lie within larger overriding collection documents, perhaps as practical appendices. This way, they can be related directly to the objectives within those documents which they support. The number and range of plans required will reflect the complexity of the collection itself and the presence (or not) of other features and vegetation. Some plans may be very simple indeed, but for most, it is useful to break the arboretum down into smaller units. By doing this, it becomes much easier to consider the overall maintenance requirement as well as the organisation and scheduling of the work required. This division may be done in various ways; it may be based on the various components of the landscape along the lines of the following:

- ▲ the trees and shrubs comprising the collection
- ▲ other vegetation—lawns, wild grass, non-collection trees and shrubs, including shelterbelts, hedges, woodland screens, etc.
- ▲ natural features—lakes, rivers, etc.
- ▲ artificial features—roads, signs, walls, built features, interpretive panels, benches, etc. (PLATE 50)

Breaking things down in this way helps greatly in the matching and allocation of the relevant tools, equipment, and skills to the jobs required. In large establishments, even the staffing structure may reflect these different components, with specialist teams dedicated to each type of work. More commonly though, arboretum staff tend to turn their hands to a range of jobs with specialist tasks being contracted out (more on staffing later in this chapter). Of course, this method in itself does not help decide on best timing or level of maintenance operations. To do this, many arboretums and gardens adopt a system of zoning according to the level of maintenance required. In this way, schedules can be prepared according to the frequency or level of maintenance work needed in each zone. Table 4 shows a zoning system in a mixed tree and shrub collection with non-collection trees and vegetation and other commonly seen features.

These zones may be any size and may even overlap each other where different plant types are interplanted or at different structural levels—a specialist shrub collection planted within a wider arboretum beneath a canopy of large specimen trees, for example.

These two methods of considering the organisation of maintenance will be suitable for different collections. Some arboretums may be quite

TABLE 4. MAINTENANCE ZONES.

MAINTENANCE LEVEL	ZONE	MAINTENANCE TASKS
Low	Natural woodland and shelterbelts	Occasional thinning or felling
	Parkland	Maintenance of fences, walls, and tree enclosures
	Wild grassland	Annual cutting
Medium	General arboretum	Regular inspections and labelling
		Regular arboricultural maintenance—crown management, mulching, etc.
		Road and path repairs
	Informal lawns	Tree removal and planting
		Monthly mowing
High	Shrubs collections	Regular pruning
	Visually important and popular visitor areas	Regular checks and high standard of maintenance
	Formal lawns	Frequent mowing, spiking, feeding

homogeneous but with a range of landscape components intimately combined. In this case zoning is unlikely to be useful, though defining the different components according to the first method may be. Others may have clearly definable zones better served by the second method.

Because of the seasonal nature of almost all gardens, it is inevitable that maintenance plans will reflect this. Many tasks, such as pruning a particular plant group, will need to be carried out during quite a narrow window of time, and even planting, hedge cutting, and other more flexible jobs will tend to be done in certain seasons. Calendars or year-planners can be useful templates for planning the cycle of maintenance for these annual jobs, with five-year planners used for tasks with a longer cycle. Shrub pruning may be a good example of this kind of job—for example, the biennial pruning of dogwoods for stem colour.

Maintenance schedules

Schedules are the final part of this maintenance planning process. They can be drawn up weekly or monthly but will be derived from the longer-term plans just outlined. They may simply be drawn periodically from the annual calendar, but in practice, weather conditions, staffing fluctuations, equipment breakdowns, and a whole range of other unpredictable factors make it necessary for scheduling of work to be flexible. This is the level of management usually organised by hands-on supervisors or even the gardeners or arborists themselves. But that doesn't mean it is less important, and many a fine plan can come to nothing if the final link in the chain is missing and work doesn't get done on the ground.

Regular inspections

However well planned a program of maintenance and renewal is, there will always be a need to inspect grounds and facilities to check their condition. Adverse weather, wear and tear, or even deliberate damage can result in the need for repair or replacement. In any garden where visitors (either paying or free) are allowed entry, inspection will be an essential part of monitoring safety and fulfilling the duty of care.

Plate 1. A miracle of natural architecture. The complex skeleton of trunk and branches can provide a source of wonder for scientists and tree lovers alike. Photo by Steve Wooster, © Forestry Commission.

Plate 2. From North America to England: *Sequoiadendron giganteum* (giant redwood) was one of many majestic conifers to be collected and returned to Europe during the mid 19th century. This one ended up gracing the sumptuous landscape of Robert Holford at Westonbirt. Photo by Steve Wooster, © Forestry Commission.

Plate 3. Botanical collectibles from South America: the monkey puzzle avenue at Bicton, Devon, UK.

Plate 4. One of the early 20th century's great plant treasures, *Davidia involucrata* (handkerchief tree) became the subject of fierce rivalry between European nurseries and their intrepid plant hunters. The genus honors French missionary Père David, whose descriptions of its immense beauty proved irresistible.

Plate 5. The streets of New York can become an arboretum with the simple addition of labels to the sidewalk trees.

Plate 6. Even a small suburban garden can accommodate a collection of trees and shrubs. Although the scale is different, the principles of selection and layout remain the same as for larger collections.

Plate 7. The entrance to the Morton Arboretum reflects its modern public role.

Plate 9. The Leominster Loop bowl depicts the fourteen trees planted in the town's millennium tree-planting project. Photo by Anna Mumford, with kind permission of the Lyon family.

Plate 8. Towns all over the world have tree-filled municipal gardens in which an arboretum can be established. Queenstown Gardens, New Zealand.

Plate 10. Trees have been planted to commemorate people and events for hundreds of years. At the National Memorial Arboretum, trees provide a natural accompaniment to the columns and other built structures. Courtesy Driftwoodimages2007.

Plate 11. Outdoor learning: a "forest classroom" established in a school playground can help to connect children with trees and the environment through many areas of study.

Plate 12. The arboretum at Keele University rubs shoulders with car parks and buildings and provides an accessible teaching resource for a variety of courses. Courtesy David Emley, Keele University Arboretum.

Plate 13. A new collection for new challenges: the Leventritt Garden at the Arnold Arboretum combines beauty with function and shows how arboretums can adapt to the needs of a changing world. Courtesy The Arnold Arboretum Archives, © President and Fellows of Harvard College.

Plate 14. Local volunteers at a Trees for Cities community planting day in Clapham Common, London. Photo by Kirsty Wedge, © Trees for Cities.

KEY

- Site boundary
- Serpentine Ride
- Path
- Road
- Woodland
- Shrub planting
- Specimen Trees (exl prop)
- Glade
- Water
- Operations
- Car Park

Harcourt Arboretum
University of Oxford Botanic Garden

Diagram with notes
213/01/104
Scale 1:4,000 @ A2
Revision A

Kim Wilkie
Associates

Plate 15. The central building of the Arnold Arboretum serves the broad range of scientific functions included in its mission statement.

Plate 16. The Harcourt Arboretum master plan shows the layout of artificial and natural features. Trees and shrubs are shown individually or as clumps, and notes provide additional information to aid interpretation. A map of this kind provides the basis for communication and planning applications. Courtesy Kim Wilkie Associates.

Plate 17. A tree collection established in an urban park. The materials and design of artificial features such as surfaced paths and benches serve their purpose and match the park's city atmosphere.

Plate 18. Whatever the season, thoughtful arrangement and grouping of trees can greatly enhance their beauty. Photo by Hugh Angus, © Forestry Commission.

Plate 19. Dense planting at Bodenham Arboretum, Worcestershire, UK. Planting at close spacing like this means that thinning will be required at a later stage to allow large specimen trees to develop fully.

Plate 20. The Gardenesque landscape of the Sheffield Botanical Gardens, UK. Expanses of grass contrast with groups of trees, positioned to allow each one to develop and be appreciated to its full potential. Courtesy Meg Jullien.

Plate 21. Contrast and scale at The National Arboretum, Westonbirt. Robert Holford, the arboretum's creator, applied the principles of the Picturesque movement to create the lavishly laid out landscape of glades and rides.

Plate 22. The hornbeam arch at Polly Hill Arboretum in West Tisbury, Massachusetts, demonstrates a novel way to use trees to create an unusual landscape feature.

Plate 23. New take on an old theme: the Oak Allee at Philadelphia's Morris Arboretum. Tree-lined drives or walkways like this first became popular in 17th- and 18th-century Europe but have been reinterpreted in many gardens and arboretums in more recent times. Courtesy Paul Meyer, Morris Arboretum.

Plate 24. A broad ride left unplanted to allow for walking and viewing at Bodenham Arboretum.

Plate 25. Maple Loop at Westonbirt Arboretum, where a collection of Japanese maples has been established beneath an open canopy of larch. The resulting woodland garden has a naturalistic feel despite the maintenance required to prevent its tumbling into weedy chaos. Photo by Hugh Angus, © Forestry Commission.

Plate 26. Plant sales area at Bodenham Arboretum. Retail opportunities like this provide valuable income but should be carefully considered to avoid an over-commercial atmosphere.

Plate 27. Seeing trees in a different light: illuminated trails have become popular events for winter time and may combine earning with an interpretive function.
© Forestry Commission.

Plate 28. The choice of what to collect is enormous: from the grandeur of large trees (*Eucalyptus delegatensis*, Christchurch Botanic Gardens, New Zealand)—

Plate 29. —to the subtle beauty of small flowering shrubs, as here, the winter flowers of witch hazel. Photo by Steve Wooster, © Forestry Commission.

Plates 30 and 31. The flowers hold the key to plant classification: a male cone of maritime pine (*Pinus pinaster*) and flower of *Magnolia stellata* 'Rosea' represent the two major plant groups, gymnosperms and angiosperms.

Plate 32. Dazzling autumn colour on *Acer palmatum* 'Osakazuki'. It may take pains-taking selection for generations of trees to produce successful cultivars like this old favourite. Courtesy Peter Gregory.

Plate 33. The gorgeous flowers of the tulip tree are the source of one of its common names. But this and other common names give no clue to its close relationship to magnolias.

Plate 34. Species choice and landscape are intimately connected: the distinctive and beautiful treescape of conifers at Bedgebury National Pinetum.

Plate 35. Cultured beauty: last seen in the wild in the early 19th century, *Franklinia alatamaha* is preserved in collections all over the world for its superb flowers.

Plate 36. A specialist collection of Japanese maples can provide a visual feast for visitors as well as a source of reference for gardeners. Photo by Steve Wooster, © Forestry Commission.

Plate 37. An ethnobotanical (thematic) collection of trees and shrubs used by the Ainu People of Hokkaido, Japan. Sapporo Botanical Gardens.

Plate 38. A tree lover's sweet shop: the garden centre is one of the best places to look for plants as well as providing an opportunity to learn and seek advice. © Forestry Commission.

Plate 39. A modern propagation facility is a big investment but allows collectors to produce plants in large numbers from various sources and types of propagules.

Plate 40. The dappled bark of London plane, *Platanus ×hispanica*. This tough city dweller came about as a fortuitous garden hybrid of American and European parents.

Plate 41. Willows grown for their attractive stem colours can be easily propagated from cuttings with no specialist equipment or techniques.

Plate 42. The dramatic forested landscape of Hokkaido, Japan. Wild areas like this can be the source of new cultivated plants, but collectors must follow strict protocols and obtain permits.

Plate 43. Seed doesn't always grow at a convenient height, and long-handled loppers are a valuable tool for any collecting trip. It also pays to be a good catch!

Plate 44. Seed comes in many kinds of packages: compared to the fleshy globes of *Pittosporum crassifolium*—

Plate 45. —the dry fruits of *Acer palmatum* need little attention post-collection. Photo by Steve Wooster, © Forestry Commission.

Plate 46. Voucher sample of *Acer distylum* taken to confirm identification of wild-collected seed. The most valuable samples include flowers or fruit.

Plate 47, right. Maintenance work is a neverending job: arboretum Friends repairing a protective cage on a young tree at Westonbirt Arboretum.

Plate 48. Relaxed maintenance: an area of new planting at Eastwoodhill Arboretum, New Zealand, showing that young trees can thrive without intensive grass cutting.

Plate 49, right. Warning signs and barriers: keeping visitors away from dangerous tree operations is an important part of safety management in any arboretum.

Plate 50, below. Many arboretums contain natural habitats that require maintenance: sward management on wildflower-rich limestone grassland.

Plate 51. Mulching young plants makes chemical weeding unnecessary and mowing easy. The stakes indicate that these shrubs require regular inspection until established.

Plate 52. Newly planted trees may need help to survive a variety of threats. Cages need to be high enough to prevent browsing by deer, rabbits, or other pests and wide enough to allow the tree to grow.

Plate 53. Badly fitted or unchecked tree stakes can rub and damage the young plants they are there to support.

Plate 54. Basic pruning technique to remove a small side branch. Branch is first shortened to reduce weight and then undercut to avoid ripping.

Plate 55. The branch is then top cut to meet the undercut.

Plate 56. The completed cut (note correct position of cut to the line of branch collar—not flush) is neat and will occlude quickly.

Plate 57. The end result of successful target pruning: the wound has healed completely.

Plate 58. To encourage a fresh supply of colourful young shoots, dogwoods should be pruned back to a short stem in early spring before bud-burst. Photo by Steve Wooster, © Forestry Commission.

Plate 59, top left. Acute forks like this become weaker and more liable to splitting with age. Early formative pruning is the best prevention.

Plate 60, top right. Without early formative pruning, young trees can quickly develop a poor branch structure and shape.

Plate 61, left. A young tree with raised crown to give a clean stem and attractive shape.

Plate 62. Pruning is often carried out for aesthetic reasons. Here, an avenue of European limes is tidied up by pruning the epicormic shoots.

Plates 63 and 64, top left and right. Big jobs need big equipment. Stump grinders and tree spades are expensive, and most collections use commercial contractors to carry out specialist operations like this.

Plate 65, bottom left. Popularity has a price: beautiful trees like this attract many admirers, and their root zones can quickly become compacted by thousands of feet.

Plate 66, bottom right. Wildlife vandals: bark-stripping by grey squirrels is a big problem in many countries, not just their native North America.

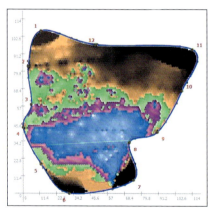

Plate 67, above. How likely to fail? A scarlet oak showing the fungal fruiting bodies of *Ganoderma* sp. is assessed with Picus tomographic equipment.
© Forestry Commission.

Plate 68, center left. Decay revealed: the tomogram produced by measuring the passage of shock waves through the trunk shows, by means of colour, the varying degrees of decay. © Forestry Commission.

Plate 69, opposite. The 400-year-old Knightwood Oak in the New Forest, UK. Veterans like this need sensitive management and protection from the heavy foot traffic of interested visitors.

Plate 70, bottom left. Labelling begins before seeds have even germinated: seed trays labelled with accession numbers and plant names.

Plate 71. Gathering vital statistics: measuring trunk diameter at 4 feet (1.3m) above ground level with a tape measure.
Photo by Steve Wooster, © Forestry Commission.

Plate 72. Measuring instruments: (left to right) double-sided tapes (standard scale on one side, direct diameter scale on the other), Vertex electronic rangefinder and height meter, Suunto clinometer.

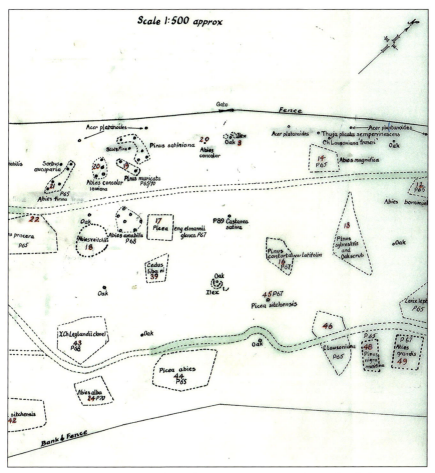

Plate 73. Mapping the traditional way: hand-drawn maps can be as detailed or as simple as necessary, with individual plants shown as dots or symbols, and clumps as representative shapes. Numbering trees is essential to relate them to the plant catalogue, and names may be added for interest. © Forestry Commission.

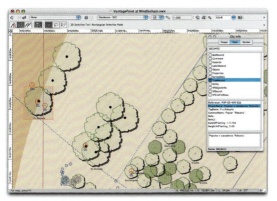

Plate 74. Geographic Information Systems combine maps with data relating to the trees or other features shown and can be viewed and edited on an office-based or handheld computer. © 2000–09 Joel M. Sciamma—Inventors Emporium & John P. Smith—Mosaic Mapping.

Plate 75. Surveying trees and landscape features using GPS technology. Under ideal conditions accuracy to less than 3 feet (1m) is possible. © 2000–09 Joel M. Sciamma—Inventors Emporium & John P. Smith—Mosaic Mapping.

Plate 76, top right. Temporary labels are cheap and can be made as they are needed in the field. They may be attached at the time of surveying or provide a backup for more informative tree labels.

Plates 77 and 78, center and bottom right. Labels can be tied to low branches or protective cages with cable ties or wire.

Plates 79 and 80, top and center left. Other means of secure attachment: labels can be screwed or nailed to trunks or a wooden post.

Plate 81, top right. The label for this young tree is carried on a plinth.

Plate 82, bottom left. A standard engraved plastic tree label showing a typical range and layout of information.

Plate 83, center right. Small, handheld label printers are ideal for producing tab labels for seed trays and plant pots.

Plate 84, top right. Tree labels are the most basic form of interpretation and the starting point for developing many visitors' interest.

Plate 85, center right. A simple plinth giving information about an individual tree. Physical features and practical uses are common areas of information for interpretive plinths of this kind, and the use of pictures is a valuable addition.

Plates 86, bottom, and 87, center left. Thematic collection of native trees at Westonbirt Arboretum. Integrated plant layout, paths, and innovative interpretive features complement one another and provide a cohesive visitor experience.

Plate 88. Arboretum entrances don't have to be grand but should give a sense of arrival. The wooden arch at the entrance to this forest arboretum sets the atmosphere for interpretive themes to be developed later.

Plate 89. The visitor centre at Eastwoodhill Arboretum, from where a range of trails, guided walks, and other interpretation start.

Plate 90. Children's interpretation at Auckland Botanic Gardens, New Zealand. Routes that invite exploration and interactive interpretive boards are popular features for children.

Plate 91. A simple route guide situated at the entrance to a small arboretum, combining a route-finding function with an introduction to the sensory trail.

This arboretum contains a small selection of trees from around the world.

Try your senses on the 6 interesting trees we have selected for you to enjoy.

YOU ARE HERE

Plate 92. Guided walks may be tailored to different age groups and ability levels: a children's guided tour at the Morris Arboretum. Courtesy Paul Meyer, Morris Arboretum.

Plate 93. An interactive plinth at Auckland Botanic Gardens, designed for children. Information plinths don't have to be dull; the elements of design, information content, and physical construction work together to deliver the interpretive objectives.

Plate 94, left. Fingerpost located at a route junction and designed with a suitable scale and materials to match its surroundings.

Plate 95, right. Even trail waymarkers can contribute to interpretive themes and become interesting features in their own right.

Plate 96. Interpretive plinth on the canopy walkway at Otari-Wilton's Bush, Wellington, New Zealand. Information is broken into bite-sized chunks, with type size and style used to differentiate basic and more detailed elements.

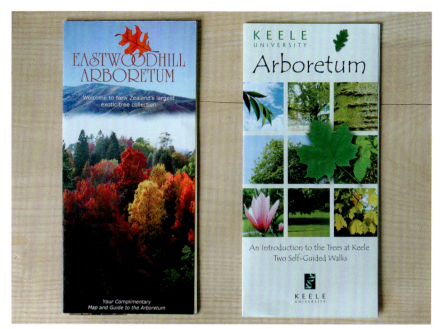

Plate 97. Two guide leaflets giving visitors basic information and suggested walking routes. This format allows them to be easily distributed via leaflet dispensers.

Plate 98. A visitor guide, with a range of colour-coded trails described. Courtesy Eastwoodhill Arboretum.

Plate 99. Whether trails are described in general or specific leaflets, permanent or temporary waymarkers are likely to be needed to complement maps.

Plate 100. A metal sculpture at Christchurch Botanic Gardens: artistic interpretations may not provide hard facts but can add a different dimension to the appreciation of plants.

Plate 101. What do trees sound like? A fun interpretive feature designed to encourage children of all ages to experiment with the sounds of wood.

Plate 102. Spoken interpretation with no wires: use of a wind-up audio gets around the need for electrical power in a remote woodland location at Westonbirt Arboretum. Photo by Steve Wooster, © Forestry Commission.

Plate 103. Visitor centres, such as this one at the Polly Hill Arboretum, can fulfil a number of interpretive functions, from information provision to sales of books and T-shirts.

Plate 104. Tree-related events may take many forms: hands-on propagation at the Morris Arboretum. Courtesy Paul Meyer, Morris Arboretum.

Plate 105. Open days can be a valuable way to demonstrate the range of skills needed to manage trees: climbing demonstration at the Morris Arboretum. Courtesy Paul Meyer, Morris Arboretum.

Plate 106. Volunteers can turn their hands to almost any job: collecting maple seeds for propagation.

In practice, inspections can usually be carried out along with the program of planned maintenance, just like the other jobs in Table 4. And like other jobs, inspections should be carried out at a frequency suited to what features are being inspected and their likely need for attention. For anything that could, if not maintained, cause injury or damage, it will be important to maintain records of inspections completed, along with any necessary work identified and the date of completion. A safety check on paths, benches, and other facilities, for example, may be carried out at the beginning of each week or month, depending on level of use.

Of particular importance in a tree collection will be the inspection of the plants themselves. These inspections may be carried out for a number of reasons, including monitoring plants for health and for visitor safety. These are both large subjects in themselves and will be dealt with later under their own headings. The important thing is that they should be covered by a regular program of inspection and recording.

Arboriculture

Maintenance of any arboretum will require a range of management techniques to match the features and vegetation in it. However, this book is far too small to consider them all, and only those relating to the collection trees and shrubs themselves will be considered. For information about general garden or parkland maintenance, readers should refer to the list of references at the back of the book.

For most tree collectors, arboriculture is the area of maintenance closest to their hearts. It is the work that will help to ensure that the collection contains well-formed, healthy trees and shrubs. The term "arboriculture" is used to describe not just the distinctive horticulture of woody plants but also the wide range of technical, legal, and environmental aspects of trees and their human interactions. The term "tree surgery," used to describe the manual tree work element of arboriculture, has become less popular in recent years; tree surgeons are now generally referred to as arborists.

At one end of the life cycle of a cultivated tree or shrub lies propagation, planting, and early tending; at the other, the associated work is of a much more physical and mechanical nature: the pruning or felling of large trees. All tasks are equally important, though the skills required are quite distinct and may require different groups of staff to carry them out. In new collections, where planting is the name of the game, large tree work may be unnecessary, whereas restoration of a neglected park or arboretum could require extensive tree removal before any new planting can even be contemplated. Staffing and maintenance plans need to acknowledge this.

Arboriculture is a large subject, so readers requiring detailed information about specific areas are advised to refer to the list of references at the back of the book.

So why do we need arboriculture? After all, trees and shrubs in the wild are perfectly able to look after themselves without the help of arborists. This is true, but trees in cultivation are not the same as wild trees, both in their origin and the expectations put upon them. For a start they may be growing in an environment or climate very different from that experienced in their natural range or forest situation. And the rate of failure seen in natural populations of trees would be quite unacceptable in cultivation. This is particularly true of collection trees that will often be rare and have had considerable resources dedicated to their collection, propagation, and planting. In addition, trees in cultivation may be expected to conform to aesthetic standards of shape and form that require pruning or training to achieve and maintain.

Having said that good arboricultural practice can improve tree survival and health, much of the work carried out under the umbrella of arboriculture has as much to do with meeting human needs and sensibility as it does to the well-being of the tree itself. The work of Alex Shigo (1991) has shown how trees adapt to and resist decay organisms and other environmental threats, and old-fashioned interventionist arboriculture, involving aggressive techniques like cavity filling and over-enthusiastic cable bracing, have been shown to act against the tree's natural capacity to adapt and may do more harm than good. But arboriculture has changed greatly in recent decades in response to this growing understanding, and a more sympathetic approach has developed that allows trees to develop and adapt naturally while still being maintained to meet human benefit. A striking example of this is the rise in appreciation of veteran trees described later in the chapter.

The following headings cover the areas of arboriculture most relevant to the maintenance of tree and shrub collections.

Planting and protection

Although the initial establishment phase of an arboretum may be the most concentrated period of planting, the need to replace lost trees and perhaps expand or develop means that it is a job that is universal to old and new collections alike. It is traditionally carried out during the dormant winter months but, by using container-grown plants and supplementary watering, planting may be extended to other times of the year.

Planting trees is not difficult, though everyone seems to have their own particular view on how it should be done. Providing a few rules are followed, anyone can plant successfully, making it a great job for involving community groups and sponsors. Nevertheless, the subject of planting is too large to be dealt with in detail in this book, and readers are advised to seek advice from more specialised publications, some examples of which are included in the references list. The following are some important principles.

- ▲ Size and quality. Obtain good-quality, healthy plants of an appropriate size (see Chapter 3). This will not only mean quicker establishment and fewer losses but will also avoid the need to stake plants for support.
- ▲ Plant handling. Handling of plants before and during planting is important to avoid damage, particularly drying out of the roots. Inexperienced planters are often unaware of the importance of keeping young roots covered and out of the sun or drying wind. Anyone organising a tree-planting event should bear this in mind and ensure that those taking part are closely supervised.
- ▲ Weed control. Control of weeds is vital to reduce competition for moisture and avoid drought-stress. New plants should be mulched with composted wood chips (to a depth of 2 inches, 5cm) or mulch

mats to control weed growth. A clear weed-free zone, 3 feet (1m) in diameter, should be maintained around the young tree until it is established. (PLATE 51)

▲ Protection. Young trees are prone to various threats from animals and careless humans. Animal pests may include deer, rabbits, or grazing stock, but cages may also help to keep over-tidy lawnmower and strimmer operators at a safe distance. Protective cages of the appropriate size should be erected at the time of planting and maintained until the tree is big enough to look after itself. (PLATE 52)

Post-planting tending

Most young trees and shrubs being planted into a collection will have come from the cosseted conditions of a nursery or propagation facility. They will have been regularly watered and protected from extremes of temperature and wind, as well as damaging animal pests. Although care will have been taken to judge when plants are sufficiently well developed to be planted out, their sudden introduction into the harsher environment of the wider arboretum can be a shock, and success will depend on early care. Establishment—the phase between planting and the point where plants can be considered independent—is the period in the life cycle of cultivated trees where the rate of failure is highest, and good practice can make a great difference. For this reason, many collections differentiate between unestablished and established plants to recognise the additional needs of young trees and shrubs. This unestablished status may be marked physically on the ground with a coloured stake or other marker or more invisibly as a database entry. Both can be removed once the young plant is considered sufficiently well established to need less frequent attention.

Young trees need their own program of maintenance and one that must be given a high level of priority. The most important part of this program will be regular inspection to identify problems before it's too late for remedial action. Watering during periods of drought and maintenance of a weed-free root zone are probably the most important considerations, but there are other things to keep an eye on, including the condition of stakes, ties, and protective cages. All these have the potential to strangle or damage a promising young plant if they're not loosened or adequately maintained. In some cases on poor soils, additional fertilisation may also be necessary, although this should not be done without good evidence of a need. Regular checks may also identify a need to carry out early pruning to encourage young trees to develop a sound and attractive shape. This so-called formative pruning can greatly reduce the need for more aggressive pruning later on. It is dealt with in more detail under the next heading, along with other kinds of pruning. (PLATE 53)

Pruning

Pruning may be carried out for a number of reasons throughout the life span of any tree or shrub. In most cases the aim is to control size or appearance, or to prevent damage to human life or property. It is important, though, not to regard pruning as an automatic necessity in most situations, but an operation used sparingly in response to specific needs. Skillful and judicious pruning can help to produce a structurally sound tree that is less liable to damage during storms and other adverse conditions. Some groups of trees may require pruning to remove diseased branches, and ornamental shrubs often benefit from regular pruning to encourage flowering or stem colour. But pruning must be carried out by skilled people with knowledge of the plants they are working with. As a general rule and where necessary, it should be started as early as possible, before the tree has had time to develop a poor form requiring removal of large limbs. Careful selection of planting stock or good nursery practice can help greatly in this respect. But even plants with a good form when planted can quickly develop forks and weak branching, and there is no substitute for regular inspections to identify and remedy problems—"nipping in the bud" is the best phrase to describe this approach!

Pruning is a large and complex subject and, although this section will describe the main types used to maintain trees, readers are advised to refer to one of the many good books specialising in the subject (see the reading list at the back of this book). Some of these references list plants by genus and provide specific guidance for each. This is particularly valuable for the diversity of shrub pruning methods.

General pruning techniques. If carried out badly, pruning can do more harm than good. The positioning of cuts is particularly important; the aim is to leave a wound that will heal quickly and reduce the likelihood of fungal infection and subsequent decay of the main stem. In addition, it is important to avoid leaving a stub or wounding or tearing the bark by careless or poor technique. For most pruning of trees, the term "target pruning" is used to describe the ideal (not flush) position of the cut. Plates 54 through 57 show the correct line and sequence of cuts.

Pruning tools. Providing pruning is carried out in good time, the only tools required will be secateurs and pruning saws. Good quality, sharp tools make a better job, and compact or folding models can be carried around easily for impromptu pruning. Occasionally though, large limbs will have to be removed, and chainsaws will be necessary. Even at this scale, the sequence of cuts shown in Plates 54 through 57 should be followed.

Timing of pruning. In general the timing of pruning for most species of trees and shrubs is not critical, and it is usually better to carry out important work at a less than ideal time than not at all. Late winter, before growth commences, or late spring through early summer are usually considered the best times, since the resulting wounds will be quickly healed by following growth. For cherries, it is important to prune in early to mid-summer, when they are most able to resist infection by the fungal disease silver leaf (*Chondrostereum purpureum*). Flowering shrubs and those grown for their colourful stems tend to be pruned at times to promote these features. Dogwood, for example, will be pruned in early spring, and mock orange shortly after flowering in early summer. Again, seek out references that give genus-by-genus details for shrub pruning times, such as Brown (2004). (PLATE 58)

Wound treatment. It was once common practice to "paint" wounds with a sealant to prevent entry of fungal spores or promote healing. Research has shown that these treatments are more likely to be counterproductive, and they are no longer recommended.

Work positioning. For small trees, work can be carried out from the ground or with short ladders. But for much of the life of a tree, pruning work in the crown requires climbing with rope and harness. This is a potentially dangerous operation requiring considerable training and skill, and mobile elevated work platforms (MEWPs) are playing an increasing role in such work. However, these machines are often better suited to urban streets and roads than gardens and arboretums where access and ground conditions can reduce their application. Choice over which method to use will depend on the particular situation and the assessment of risk (see "Health and Safety at Work," later in this chapter).

Crown management. This broad category of pruning involves the removal of live and dead limbs to meet various aesthetic and practical objectives. The various descriptions that follow can be useful in defining the specific work required when writing contracts for tree work.

Formative pruning. As the name suggests, this is pruning used early in the tree's life to encourage good form. It requires knowledge of the way trees grow in order to spot and correct faults that could develop and cause problems later. In addition, trees and shrubs can, to some extent, be trained to develop a desired shape for aesthetic purposes. However, this should not be overemphasised as no amount of pruning can persuade a tree or shrub to adopt a shape that is alien to its natural tendency. As mentioned earlier, formative pruning should be started in the nursery and continued as part of post-planting tending. Of particular importance at this stage is the removal of forking branches that will, if left, become weak and split, leaving a large open wound. (PLATES 59 AND 60)

Crown raising. Removal of low branches can be carried out for aesthetic and practical purposes. It is particularly suited to trees and larger shrubs that naturally (or for ornamental reasons) have a clean trunk. It allows easier mowing and weed control around the base of the tree and can enhance the effect of attractively coloured or textured bark. On the downside, if used as a standard prescription for all trees regardless of their natural form, it can give a rather artificial or formal appearance to a landscape. The immaculately pruned "lollipop" trees seen in formal gardens of the 18th century prove this point. Likewise, increasing mechanisation of garden maintenance and the need for vehicular access should not be allowed to dictate an overzealous pruning of low limbs and the loss of variety and character.

Crown raising of conifers is often called brashing. It is a technique used by foresters to produce knot-free timber, but the same technique can be used by gardeners to create a bare-trunked specimen. It is particularly suitable for conifers grown in close groups where shading has resulted in the death of the low branches. For a really dramatic effect, long-handled pruning saws can be used to produce a clean trunk of 15 feet (4.5m) or more. (PLATE 61)

Crown reduction. The result of this type of pruning is an overall reduction in the crown volume by shortening of branches back to side shoots. The overall effect is a more compact crown, and the technique is particularly useful where a tree is considered to be taking up too much room or encroaching on others around it. Because branches are being shortened at the crown's margin, care must be taken not to create an unnatural-looking or ugly outline. Drastic lopping of trees that have become too big demonstrates this and emphasises the need to avoid poor species choice in the first place. In general, a 30 percent reduction in the crown area should be considered a maximum.

Crown thinning. This involves the removal of limbs from within the crown to reduce its density. It is carried out to open a congested crown or one containing rubbing, dead, or damaged branches. It can also be used to allow greater light penetration where shading is a problem or to reduce wind resistance in a tree considered to be at risk of instability in high winds. As with crown reductions, pruning should not be too drastic, and again, 30 percent is commonly considered a maximum for most species. In practice, crown pruning is often a combination of thinning and reduction, the extent of each depending on the objectives.

Crown cleaning and deadwooding. This is the removal of deadwood, broken limbs, or unwanted vegetation, such as ivy. It may be done for safety or aesthetic reasons, but with greater awareness of the value of deadwood habitats for wildlife, the possibility of leaving dead limbs should always be considered (see "Conservation and Environmental Considerations," later in this chapter).

Epicormics and suckers. Some kinds of trees naturally produce shoots directly from the trunk or limbs, often in response to stress. These so-called epicormic shoots may be considered unsightly and, where necessary, should be removed. Where shoots arise from ground level or below, they are called suckers. If left uncontrolled they can form a thicket at the base of a tree, encroaching on neighbouring plants and colonising lawns. Many species have a habit of suckering and, where space allows, they may be left to demonstrate this natural habit. Where suckers can't be accommodated, they should be regularly cut or mown off. It is important not to use herbicides as a means of control as these can be translocated to the parent tree, possibly leading to its death. (PLATE 62)

Pollarding and coppicing. These are traditional methods of harvesting broadleaved trees and shrubs by repeated cutting of shoots back to previously cut stumps, or "knuckles." The difference between them is simply the height at which the cut is made: coppicing is at ground level, pollarding at a greater height on a short trunk, or bolling. Both methods may be applied to garden trees and shrubs for ornamental purposes. Willows, dogwoods, and even eucalyptus are common examples, the frequency of cutting determined by the desired effect. It is important not to confuse these methods with extreme crown reduction, or topping, of mature trees with no history of regular cutting. Most species are not suited to coppicing or pollarding, and many are likely to be killed by such action. In particular, very few conifers respond to drastic pruning like this.

Bracing and propping

This is the use of artificial support to strengthen or reduce the risk of failure of the whole tree or an individual limb or fork. Bracing is less common than it once was, partly due to the expense and need for frequent inspection and monitoring following installation. Overuse of bracing can also undermine the natural ability of trees to respond to weakness. Modern, flexible systems have largely overcome this concern, but bracing should be reserved for special circumstances or to extend the safe life of trees with exceptional historical or botanical value.

Tree removal

Unlike forestry, tree removal in the arboretum often involves gradual dismantling rather than complete felling. As well as the likelihood of damaging nearby features like roads, buildings, and services, there will probably be other specimens that must be avoided and make felling impossible. Climbing by rope and harness or use of a MEWP are the only ways to go about dismantling such a tree, with trunk and limbs dropped or lowered in sections. This is a slower and more expensive process than whole-tree felling, but one benefit is that the work of handling and chipping branches and larger elements can be done systematically as they are dropped from the tree.

Management of arisings

Even a modest-sized tree collection will produce a lot of wood through pruning and removals. The term "arisings" is used to describe this plant material and, although some may be sold or used internally as firewood, most will be low-value small-dimension branch wood. Disposal of this material as waste can be expensive and, more importantly, environmentally wasteful or damaging. It's far better to utilise it within the arboretum, and the start of the process is usually chipping. Chippers come in a variety of sizes, self-powered or tractor-driven. Small gardens or arboretums may choose to contract this work to a company, but this brings with it potential problems of storage and double handling of bulky material until the next visit from the chipper. For this reason, all but the smallest collections usually choose to own a chipper, and it tends to be one of the most used pieces of equipment in the arboretum. Once produced, the chip may be used for surfacing rustic paths or even play areas, but for the rest, the best option is to use it as mulch. But there is a potential problem with this. The arisings from the maintenance of woody plants is rather different from that produced in herbaceous plant collections. In particular the nutrient (especially nitrate) level of chipped wood and branches, even when it includes the leaves, is low. This means that organisms (mainly fungi and bacteria) breaking down the woody carbon component tend to rob nutrients from elsewhere to make up for the deficiency. This makes freshly chipped material unsuitable for using as mulch around trees since it has the potential to create an acute nutrient deficiency in the surrounding soil. This is indicated by yellowing of the leaves or even death of the tree. Woody waste therefore needs to be composted to a point where it no longer poses this threat.

Composting woody waste

Unfortunately, turning woody waste into compost is not quite as simple as just piling it up and waiting for nature to take its course. As well as a certain amount of turning to be done, there are a number of potential problems. For a start, the run-off from a compost heap is likely to be harmful if it reaches a stream or river, and so care must be taken to control it. In addition, though heat is an essential part of successful composting, too high a temperature can result in spontaneous combustion. The conclusion to this is that composting needs to be carefully considered and planned. The site chosen must allow for regular turning to regulate temperature and allow all the material to be broken down evenly. In practice, the best facilities use a series of bays containing waste at progressively more advanced stages of composting. Each is turned into the next one in line as it reaches the next stage of decomposition. The time taken from start to finish varies depending on a number of factors, including size of chip, temperature and moisture levels, and the amount of leaf or other material containing more nitrogen. The last factor can make a marked difference, and in mixed gardens of herbaceous and woody plants, arisings may be combined before composting to speed up the process. As a rule, the process takes three to twelve months, and composting is complete when turning the heap is no longer followed by a rise in temperature.

Stump removal

There is no automatic necessity to remove stumps, and in certain, more naturalistic settings, they can become a feature. However, stumps get in the way of mowing and other ground work, and in a more tended landscape they can be visually intrusive. If there are a lot of them, they may also limit the number of potential planting sites, though new plants can be put quite close to removed ones with no ill effect. Where removal is the chosen option, there are two methods: complete removal and grinding to beneath ground level. The former is quite feasible with small trees that can be pulled out with a relatively small tractor or winch. But for large trees, substantial equipment and excavation is needed, and the result is considerable disturbance to the surrounding soil. For this reason, large tree stumps are usually removed with a stump grinder. These come in a variety of sizes and, as with most machinery, there is a trade-off between size and manoeuvrability. Small self-powered models are great for tight situations and help to avoid compaction, but they struggle with large stumps. Stumps should be ground to about 12 inches (30cm) below the level of the surrounding land to allow reinstatement of the grass, but care must be taken where other trees are growing nearby not to damage their roots. (PLATE 63)

Moving trees

From time to time and for various reasons it may be necessary to move established trees. Up to a certain size, this can be done by hand-digging round the root plate and moving as much root and soil as possible with the help of a sack or sheeting. But once a tree gets too large to be manhandled in this way, the job becomes one for mechanical equipment, such as a tree spade. This is a specialist job, and it is best to bring in a contractor with the machinery and experience to carry it out. As with tree planting, it is best done during the dormant season. (PLATE 64)

Mulching and soil maintenance

Tree growing is a very benign activity compared to many other land uses, and trees generally take and return nutrients to the soil in a slow and largely wasteless cycle. But without some consideration for the trees' physiological needs, careless management can lead to a gradual deterioration in soil quality.

It is an obvious statement that good soil conditions are fundamental to the growth and well-being of the plants growing in them. Nutrient status, pH, physical structure, water retention, and a host of other factors contribute to what we call soil quality. In most cases, little can be done to change the nature of the underlying soil except to choose a different place to start your collection! But certain actions can be taken to help maintain the structure and fertility of the soil. In particular, reducing (or relieving) compaction and minimising unnecessary removal of nutrients from the soil are valuable contributions. In most cases leaves need not be removed but left to decay and return their nutrients to the soil and, where possible, arisings should be composted for use as mulch. As well as feeding the soil, both these measures can help to maintain the level of organic matter in the soil and improve its water retention capacity. Compacted soils pose problems for trees for a number of reasons; the lack of pores reduces the soil's capacity to absorb and retain water, and rain may be shed quickly with little getting to the roots. In addition, hard, compacted soils prevent root penetration and reduce the rate of exchange of oxygen and waste gases to and from the roots. Symptoms of compaction may be difficult to differentiate from those of other stresses and illnesses; trees usually show a general lack of vigour with sparse or undersized leaves and poor growth. Diagnosis is therefore usually circumstantial. The most common cause of compacted soils is traffic of vehicles and people. Some soils (particularly clays) are more liable to compaction than others, and the situation is exacerbated by wet conditions. Once soils have become compacted, it can be difficult and expensive to remedy, so by far the best way to fight compaction is prevention. The use of lighter machinery or vehicles with low-impact tyres helps, along with avoiding potentially damaging operations when the soil is wet and more vulnerable. Where foot traffic may be a problem, careful planning of access routes is the best answer. "No Entry" signs and barriers are never a good feature in a garden; it's much better to use clump-planting and development of "desire routes" to guide people where you want them to go.

Where, despite best intentions, compaction has become a problem, there are various techniques designed to reverse it. So-called radial mulching uses a high pressure air gun (or air spade) to blast channels up to 12 inches (30cm) deep in a radial pattern outward from the trunk. The channels are backfilled with sandy soil, grit, or light compost. Another method, Terravention, uses compressed nitrogen injected deep into the soil to fracture and expand the soil to improve drainage and aeration; the operation may be combined with a mycorrhizal inoculation to improve nutrient supply. Both these methods are untested over a long period and are expensive to use. Even where they are effective, their benefits may take some time to become apparent and will rely on prevention of re-compaction by the initial source. (PLATE 65)

Weed control

The earlier heading on planting describes the importance of weed control for young trees. Maintenance of a weed-free rooting zone by mulching or chemical weeding is an important part of early tending and should continue until the tree is established. From this point on, weed control is unnecessary for the plant's well-being and becomes an aesthetic exercise. In fact, mowing and strimming becomes a common source of injury to young trees as soon as their protective cages are removed and their delicate stems exposed to the risk of over-tidy garden staff! The only answer is to keep machinery well away and, where it is considered unacceptable to allow long grass to develop around the base of trees, mulching or chemical weeding is the best way to achieve this. Care should be taken with the latter however as some pesticides applied over the rooting zone can damage even mature trees. Strimmers with nylon lines are often wrongly considered harmless to trees, but they can damage the trunks of even quite thick-barked trees and undo the good work of many years. Keep them away!

Disease and pest control

By their nature, tree collections usually include species growing outside their natural range. Some of these will be less than perfectly adapted to the climate and range of pests and diseases they encounter in their artificial environment. Fighting disease with pesticides is rarely a satisfactory solution for environmental and practical reasons, and by far the best way to prevent problems is to maintain healthy populations of trees by good horticultural practice. This is partly a question of selecting healthy plants (see Chapter 3) and avoiding those species that do not thrive in the ambient conditions. An example is the growing of northern species of birch in the warmer regions of the USA, where they become very prone to insect borers and fungal disease. Matching plants to suitable soil and other conditions, including shade and exposure, are also important considerations.

The pathology of trees and shrubs is a very large subject. Readers wishing for more information on specific diseases or pests should refer to one of the specialist books listed in the reference section at the back of the book.

Health inspections. Regular inspection for and reporting of illness is an important part of managing any plant collection. Some diseases may be spotted during routine work, but there is no substitute for someone with knowledge carrying out systematic inspection. Some diseases or pest infestations will require rapid action for hygiene reasons while others may prompt a program of control to minimise the impact. A plant badly affected by fire blight should be removed and destroyed quickly, whereas a group of cherries with blossom wilt may be identified for annual summer pruning to manage the disease. Some diseases and pests are sufficiently serious to require reporting to government authorities. Preventing spread of specific diseases into the collection may require precautions such as quarantining of new plants or even exclusion of particularly susceptible genera altogether.

Animal pests. Every country has its native and non-native animal pests of trees. The question of control depends on weighing the pros and cons—the level of damage versus the adverse results of control. It may be that the animal in question is protected by law, in which case damage limitation is possible only by caging the tree or completely fencing the whole or part of the arboretum. Where control is legal and possible, the reaction of visitors may have to be taken into consideration. Grey squirrels are a big problem in European arboretums but are often loved (and even fed!) by visitors, and control measures must be managed sensitively. In these circumstances some methods may be more practical than others. Shooting may be carried out during periods of closure and to avoid the presence of hoppers containing poisonous bait. (PLATE 66)

Tree safety management

The general matter of occupier's liability has been dealt with earlier in the chapter, along with the need to inspect grounds and features for safety reasons. In an arboretum containing middle-aged and mature trees, one of the potential hazards are the trees themselves. Adverse weather, disease, and a number of other less common factors can lead to deterioration in a tree's stability or structural strength that may go unnoticed without careful observation. The risk posed should not be overemphasised, since the frequency of injury arising from limb shedding or wind-blow is extremely low. However, these risks should be considered and an appropriate level of inspection used to identify hazards and, where necessary, prompt remedial work. Just how frequent and detailed these inspections need to be depends on various factors, including the size and condition of the trees present and the number of visitors. A large old tree overhanging a visitor centre is going to need a more frequent and thorough inspection than a small one in a quieter location. For this reason, most arboretums adopt a system of zoning according to level of usage or the presence of buildings or other targets. Table 5 is typical.

An accompanying map of the grounds will show the layout of the zones for those carrying out the work. Within the zones each tree must

TABLE 5. TYPICAL ZONING SYSTEM AND INSPECTION REGIME.

ZONE	DESCRIPTION	INSPECTION LEVEL
1 = high risk	Within tree-falling distance of main roads, paths, buildings, and other busy visitor areas	Annual inspections (or more frequently where special conditions require it)
2 = medium risk	Quiet paths, glades, and other less busy areas	5-yearly inspections
3 = low risk	Remote and very quiet areas including woodland and shelterbelt	Inspections only following reported problems

be inspected according to the likely level of risk it poses. Obviously a young healthy tree with no visible faults will require far less attention than a large one with a complex branch structure and signs of decay. The level of skill required by the inspector will also vary accordingly.

Tree inspection is a complex subject requiring knowledge of tree physiology and pathology. Those readers wishing to study the subject in more depth should read one of the books specialising in the subject. In particular, *The Principles of Tree Hazard Assessment and Management* (Lonsdale 1999) gives comprehensive advice on all aspects of tree safety management. Many owners and managers of gardens and arboretums employ arboricultural consultants to carry out their inspections for them. Others choose to perform basic inspections with their own staff while passing more advanced work to specialists. The basis of tree safety management is so-called Visual Tree Inspection (VTA). This involves a systematic visual investigation of the tree's health and structure for signs of weakness. Inspections are best carried out in early autumn, when the fruiting bodies of potentially damaging fungi are most likely to be present. They are usually carried out from the ground with the aid of binoculars and a few simple tools such as mallets and probes for investigating cavities or areas of decay. For most trees, this level of inspection is sufficient to make a judgment on the need for any remedial work or removal. It is also the level that can often be carried out by internal staff with some additional training in tree inspection.

In some cases external signs such as cracks or bulges may require a higher level of inspection to provide more information before a decision can be made. This may require climbing to get a better look at the problem or more knowledge of the subject. The presence of a fungal bracket may suggest internal decay, but judgment about whether it is a damaging species and the likely extent of the decay may be more difficult to assess. In cases like this, the opinion of a specialist may be sought. In addition to their specific subject knowledge (and insurance), arboricultural consultants may use a range of techniques and equipment developed to help indicate the extent and nature of the decay. Traditionally these techniques have relied on drilling into the trunk or affected area to measure the soundness of the wood. In recent years, more sophisticated, non-invasive methods have been introduced. An example is the

Picus tomograph, which produces a decay "map" of the inside of the tree by measuring the speed of shock waves passing through the wood. (Plates 67 and 68)

Although these techniques may provide valuable information, they require careful interpretation before a decision can be arrived at. However reliable the findings, determining the appropriate remedial work (if any) will depend on an assessment of risk. Striking a balance between safety and tree preservation is partly subjective—though quantitative assessments have been developed—and caution should be taken to avoid unnecessary removal or crown reduction through overestimating the risk posed or fear of litigation. With valuable trees in particular, removal should be considered the last resort. Figure 2 shows a flow chart for deciding the best option for remedial work.

Staffing and Human Resources

In all enterprises requiring organisation and management, the most important resource is the human one. The people that manage a garden or arboretum tend to develop a strong affinity with and loyalty to the place they work and often stay for many years, if not for their entire careers. An established team of committed workers not only fulfils the essential function of maintenance and development, but also becomes an important part of the landscape, contributing greatly to the "sense of place" and atmosphere. Their particular qualities will, inevitably, be expressed through their work to the grounds and trees they plant and maintain, so selection and retention of good staff is a fundamental element of success. In practice, members of staff in all but the largest, well-staffed arboretums tend to turn their hands to a number of different jobs, so adaptability is a great quality to look for.

Again, maintaining an arboretum has much in common with that of other gardens; but despite the similarities, the management of trees is distinctive in a number of ways from that of smaller plants, and many of the skills required may be unfamiliar to those with general horticultural or gardening training. It is for this reason that the discipline of arboriculture has developed.

FIGURE 2. DECISION FLOW CHART FOR REMEDIAL WORK ON TREES
(adapted from Lonsdale 1999).

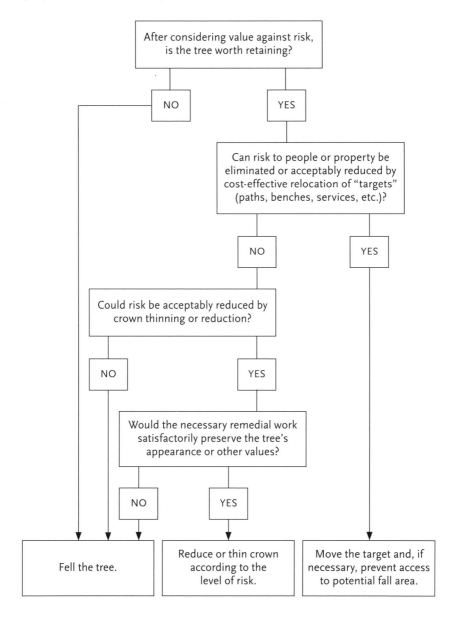

Employees and contractors

The number of staff and range of skills required to manage a tree collection depends on a number of factors. Size is, of course, among the most significant, but even quite large arboretums may have modest staff requirements for their general day-to-day grounds and tree maintenance. It is often the occasional, developmental or restorative types of work that require larger numbers of staff. Small private collections are frequently managed by the owner with a professional arborist brought in to carry out occasional large tree work. This formula is often adopted in larger institutions where the most economic solution to cover "business as usual" as well as more occasional or discrete projects is often a combination of direct and contract labour. Each has its advantages and disadvantages, as Table 6 shows, and inappropriate match of staffing to the job can be expensive or lead to a number of other problems. Finding the optimum balance requires a careful consideration of the nature and quantity of, and fluctuations in the requirement for, maintenance or other work.

TABLE 6. STAFFING: DIRECT VERSUS CONTRACT.

	DIRECT EMPLOYEES	CONTRACTORS/INDIRECT EMPLOYEES
Loyalty	Strong commitment to and association with the arboretum	Probably less loyalty Less likely to adapt to new or urgent jobs
Flexibility	Long-term commitment to employment and the expenses associated	Flexibility—hire as needed and when finance available
Rate of pay	Lower hourly/weekly rate of pay Higher peripheral costs—pensions, etc.	Higher hourly pay but no peripheral costs
Work practices	Opportunity to develop specific style or work practice for staff	May have to accept contractor's standard work practice or style
Management costs	Risk assessment, insurance cover, etc., to be dealt with in-house	Risk assessment, insurance cover by contractor—but make sure they have it!

As well as quantitative fluctuations in the staff required, there will also be specialist jobs requiring skills or qualifications not possessed by most gardeners or arborists, and expensive to obtain. Again, a judgment must be made whether it is more economic to carry out this work in-house or pay a contractor. An example of this may be the use of sophisticated decay detection for tree safety. As well as the specific skills required to interpret the results, the equipment itself will be expensive to buy for what may be only occasional use.

Volunteers

By their nature, tree collections tend to attract an enthusiastic band of supporters, many of whom may want to be directly involved in maintenance jobs. Development of volunteer groups can provide an ideal means of allowing these people to express their support and make a useful contribution. In many arboretums, particularly publicly owned ones, volunteers represent a large part of the workforce and may even have paid staff dedicated to their supervision. But volunteers should not be considered a source of free labour or an automatic replacement for paid staff. They require training, supervision, tools and equipment, and all the other support needed by regular staff and are unlikely to bring the same level of skills. On the other hand, they work by choice and frequently demonstrate a level of commitment and enthusiasm at least on a par with paid employees. In addition, a community of volunteers can become a vocal and influential force in support of the collection and a safeguard for its future.

Students and interns

Many large collections supplement their regular staff numbers with temporary student positions. These interns are often paid an allowance and may be given accommodation. As well as providing a flexible source of labour, they often bring with them new approaches to work and a healthy questioning attitude. Some collections reward their students with training opportunities, and many former interns are later recruited as permanent staff.

Skills and training

In plant collections where trees represent only a minor component, staff skills are generally weighted toward general horticulture. But as we have seen earlier, maintaining a tree collection involves some kinds of work that require specialist skills not possessed by most gardeners. This is a fact that is dealt with differently in different gardens, depending on the amount of large tree work required. Some small collections buy-in arboricultural services to carry out all their large tree work while employing direct staff with a wide variety of other skills to carry out planting, tending, and general grounds maintenance. Others have specialist groups within their staff structure to perform different areas of work. The Royal Botanic Gardens at Kew, for example, has a specialist group of arborists to maintain the arboretum trees, even though these are often intimately arranged among the beds of herbaceous plants. Most arborists work in urban environments and are engaged in growing trees for general amenity reasons, but their skills are easily adapted to the context of a botanical collection, even though the range and diversity of species will be quite different.

Arboricultural skills are often covered by specific qualifications, or tickets. Many countries have training bodies charged with the role of setting and monitoring standards for training and assessing competency in certain work tasks and the use of machinery used to carry them out. This is especially true for operations and machinery with a risk of injury or damage to health. In the UK the National Proficiency Training Council (NPTC) "promotes competence and professionalism in the workforce of the land-based and related industries by the encouragement of continuous learning and the recognition of skill." The council works with colleges and other training providers to develop training programs as well as administering a range of certification schemes for operations and machinery. An example is the use of chainsaws (CS), where a graded scheme of certification reflects the various levels of training and proficiency required for different jobs. Each qualification is numbered as follows:

CS 30   Maintenance of chainsaws and cross cutting
CS 31   Felling small trees
CS 32   Felling medium-sized trees
CS 33   Felling large trees
CS 38   Climbing trees and performing aerial tree rescue
CS 39   Operating the chainsaw from a rope and harness

Equivalent ranges of certificates cover other operations, from application of pesticides to operation of wood chippers and stump grinders.

These kinds of qualifications have become an accepted part of staff development and management and the growing requirement to manage risk. As a result, many employers consider them to be a minimum standard for their staff and even the contractors they employ.

As well as skills training and qualifications for specific operations, many countries have general arboricultural qualifications, often administered by leading bodies in the industry. In the USA, the International Society of Arboriculture (ISA) awards the Certified Arborist award to those passing its examination. This award has gained recognition in the UK, along with other qualifications, including the Technician's Certificate in Arboriculture and the Professional Diploma in Arboriculture. As well as indicating a level of competence in an individual employee, these qualifications may be a useful sign when selecting contractors.

The arboricultural industry has traditionally attracted its fair share of untrained and uninsured operators, and the minimum precaution before employing anyone should be to check they have some recognised qualification for the job. In the UK, companies that can demonstrate high standards of quality and competence may also apply for Approved Contractor status, an accreditation scheme administered by the Arboricultural Association. There are equivalent standards for arboricultural consultants both in the UK and USA: the Arboricultural Association Registered Consultant scheme, and membership of the American Society of Consulting Arborists, respectively.

Tools and machinery

Much of the equipment required to care for a tree collection will be that commonly seen in all gardens: general hand tools, mowers, light off-road vehicles for carrying people and materials, etc. There may also be more specialist equipment related to the maintenance of large trees, including MEWPs, stump grinders, and a range of chainsaws. The need for these latter kinds of tools will depend largely on the maturity of the collection and the need for large tree work. As with finding the best balance between direct employees and contract labour, similar questions arise when dealing with tools. For example, unless a stump grinder is being used week in, week out, it may be a more economic option to contract the service to a company specialising in this work rather than buying the machinery required.

Health and Safety at Work

Arboriculture is one of the most hazardous occupations, and tree work, just like that of other industries, is covered by legislation relating to occupational health and safety. In the USA this legislation is overseen by the Occupational Safety and Health Administration (OSHA); in the UK the equivalent agency is the Health and Safety Executive (HSE). General and specific information relating to arboricultural operations can be obtained from these organisations. The fundamental elements of managing health and safety in the arboretum include careful planning of operations, appropriate training, personal protective equipment (helmets, ear defenders, etc.), signage, and a range of other measures. Risk assessment is an essential prerequisite of operational work to ensure that hazards have been identified and considered along with the appropriate measures to mitigate risks. It is important that arboretum workers support a culture of health and safety and that responsibility for maintaining safe working practices is clearly defined in a health and safety policy and shared throughout the staff structure.

Conservation and Environmental Considerations

No collection of trees exists in isolation to its surrounding environment and the plants and animals that inhabit it. It is likely that principles of conservation and sustainability will be clearly identified in the mission statement and accompanying objectives, and these should be expressed right through to the day-to-day maintenance practices. This may be as simple as timing operations like scrub clearance to avoid the bird nesting season or avoiding herbicide use in wild grassland areas. Principles may be more general or based on an overall philosophy—the use of biodegradable lubricants, non-peat-based composts, or recyclable plastic products, for example. Some of these standards may be set internally, while others will be governed by legal requirements. Managers of tree collections may need to consider the following, for example:

▲ Tree Preservation Orders, felling licences
▲ wildlife conservation legislation and specific regulations—bats, birds, and other protected species
▲ habitat conservation legislation—protected area designations, nature reserves, sites of special interest, etc.
▲ chemical legislation—handling and use of pesticides and other hazardous substances

The preservation of trees is unlikely to be a difficult area for a tree collection except where development requiring felling is contemplated. Where this is the case, checks should be made that the trees concerned are not protected by law and a felling licence is not required. Potential conflicts with wildlife are not uncommon, and care must be taken not to overlook protected (or even unprotected) species during maintenance of the trees. At one level, this is a matter of avoiding damage to wildlife or their habitats but, more positively, trees may be managed to promote their well-being and that of the wildlife they support. Avoiding damage to a bat roost is a legal requirement and valuable enough, but the next step is to adopt bat-friendly tree management methods.

This may include putting up roosting boxes or maintaining suitable areas of unkempt vegetation for their insect prey.

Veteran trees

One of the most valuable and often overlooked habitats in the well-tended garden or arboretum is very old and declining trees. Managed sensitively (and with due attention to safety) trees like this can acquire great character and become favourite features in an arboretum. These so-called veterans often provide a complex "landscape" of cavities and dead or dying wood that shelters and feeds a diverse range of fungi, insects, and other creatures. Many of these organisms are highly specialised and have become increasingly uncommon due to over-tidy tree management, such as deadwooding and clearing away fallen limbs and trunks. (PLATE 69)

5 ▲ Keeping Track of the Trees
Cataloguing, Mapping, and Labelling

Perhaps the most important aspect of a tree collection, and one that sets it apart from a park or other kind of tree-covered landscape, is its cataloguing and mapping. Without the former to provide accurate information about the plants and the latter to help locate them on the ground, much of the value of any tree collection is lost. As well as being a vital tool for staff engaged in curation and management, records provide visitors and others interested in the collection with the information they need to understand and appreciate it. The extent and level of detail required of records depends very much on the collection's objectives, especially its aspirations for science, education, and research. For those collections established for ornamental purposes or personal interest, it may be enough simply to record the plants' names with reference numbers to locate their positions on a hand-drawn plan of the garden or arboretum. But when it comes to collections with ambitious aims to contribute to conservation of an endangered species or provide reference material for botanists engaged in research, a far greater level and complexity of cataloguing will be necessary. In addition, reliable labelling of plants throughout their lives, from seed to mature specimen, not only helps those wishing to identify them but also provides a link to additional data relating to them kept elsewhere in a database.

In all the areas covered in this chapter, there have been technological developments in recent years. Mapping techniques have rapidly become more sophisticated with global positioning systems (GPS) and electronic mapping replacing conventional surveying and plotting techniques. Computer databases have become the standard recording medium as cheaper and more user-friendly programs have been introduced. Palmtop and weatherproof computers mean that collecting data in the garden or on a collecting expedition can be done without the need for a clipboard and paper! Even label production has been streamlined with computer-linked engraving machines and small, handheld label printers. And it is not just large botanical gardens and arboretums that can benefit from these developments. For a small investment, even small collections can record and map their plants using modern media and disseminate information about their plants via a Web site.

Cataloguing

Chapter 3 dealt with making clear and objective choices about what species or cultivars to collect through an accession plan. As the plan is realised and plants are acquired, they must be entered into a catalogue, which will provide the structure for all the information held about them in a logical and systematic way. The first part of cataloguing plants is to allocate them a unique number.

Numbering

All collections require a system of cataloguing to provide order and easy access to the information relating to the items contained in them. Collections of trees and shrubs are no different, whether they are planted in systematic order or some other thematic or ornamental arrangement. The first part of this cataloguing is the allocation of a unique number to distinguish individual plants (or a number of indistinguishable ones) from all others, however similar. This number is generally referred to as the accession number, and it provides the link between the actual plant and all other recorded information relating to it. It is essential that this link not be broken by misallocation of data or labelling errors, since it may be difficult to reestablish at a later date. In most collections, the accession number is made up of two parts: the year of accession and a serial number. For example: 2005/0675. This accession is the 675th in the year 2005. Note the 0 in front of 675 for consistent data entry (more on databases later in the chapter). In combination, these two numbers provide a unique reference.

Depending on how plants are obtained, numbering may take place in the field at the time they are collected or as they are accepted from donors or growers. The important thing is to do it as early as possible, before they become confused with other plants entering the collection. These new plants may come in singly, in batches of identical plants, or as propagules (seeds, cuttings, etc.). In the latter cases, it is important to allocate accession numbers before seeds germinate, cuttings strike, or grafts take in order that records of those procedures (methods used and rates of success) can be catalogued. Once accessioned and numbered, immediate labelling is essential to prevent confusion and ensure that the link between accession number and plants is maintained. (PLATE 70)

The golden rule of cataloguing is not to reuse the same accession number even when the original plant has died or is no longer in the collection. Failure to do this greatly increases the possibilities for confusion, and even records of dead or removed plants should be kept for future reference under their original accession number.

Where existing parkland or urban street trees are being recorded for the first time, the process will be similar, though surveying may be carried out simultaneously with recording and labelling. In this case, although the trees are already present, the term "accessioning" can still be used to indicate that they are being formally brought into a collection. Sometimes, previously catalogued collections are recatalogued under a new or improved system. The important consideration is to link the old numbering with the new accession numbers to provide a clear link until the whole process is completed.

Single and multiple plant accessions. In many cases, accession numbers will be a reference for single plants. This is the case where individual plants are bought from nurseries or given by other collections or gardens. But often, and particularly where seeds or other propagules are being accessioned, an accession number may be allocated to a batch or many individuals. This is permissible provided all the plants or propagules are accessioned together and meet all the following criteria:

▲ all are of the same taxon (botanical name)
▲ all come from the same source—parent plant or clone
▲ all are of the same propagule type—seed, cutting, etc.

At a later date, once the plants are planted out into the collection, this multiple numbering may create a problem of distinguishing between the various individuals from a single accession. This is particularly true with trees and shrubs, which are more likely than small herbaceous species to be planted separately rather than in discrete groups within a bed or clump. To overcome the resulting ambiguity and allow mapping and other recording to distinguish between individuals, there needs to be an addition to the accession number. There are two common ways to do this.

In the first, an additional qualifier is added to the accession number for each individual; for example, the two individuals from accession 2005/0675 may be given 2005/0675A and 2005/0675B.

A second system of garden numbering may be used to uniquely identify the individual plants. This may be based on garden location—perhaps bed numbers, or numbered subdivisions of the arboretum. An important requirement of this system is that the garden numbers are clearly and securely linked to the original accession number in the database. Using the earlier example, the two individuals from accession 2005/0675 may become 23.0968 and 23.0969. Both were planted in area 23 and given the next two serial numbers in that area. They may be widely separated or close together. They will both retain their original accession number along with all the records relating to it without the need for a qualifier.

Each method has its advantages and disadvantages and works better in different situations. The first is simpler (with only one numbering system) but can lead to confusion where plants from a single accession are split, pooled, or die. In particular, where an individual plant dies or is removed, it is important that staff members responsible for records do not erroneously assume that all plants of that accession have gone and record them accordingly in the database.

The second method requires a second set of numbers, but once established, there is little room for confusion. It also allows the number to become a useful indicator of location.

What to record

In addition to accession numbers, there are three basic elements of information required for cataloguing a collection whatever its size and diversity. Each accession number should (at a minimum) be accompanied by the following information: plant name, source (where it came from), and location in the garden. For many small collections or those with modest aspirations, this level of recording is sufficient, but for most, a range of other information will be recorded. Much of this additional information is refinement and development of these three basic elements, but there are many other kinds of information covering all aspects of a tree's appearance, physical characteristics, or management that may be recorded.

The important thing when developing a system of record keeping is to consider why information is being collected and recorded, and keep things as simple as possible. Collecting large amounts of complex and detailed data is expensive and doesn't necessarily add to the collection's value unless it has some purpose. The nature and intensity of recording should be closely linked to the collection's objectives, and the allocation of staff and other resources should reflect its relative importance. Table 7 (pages 128 and 129) summarises the range of other information most commonly recorded.

Identification, naming, and verification. The standard way to name trees in a collection, just like any other plants, is by their botanical names. Common names may also be recorded, but since they are by no means standardised or internationally accepted, they should not be used as the standard reference. The subject of nomenclature is covered in more detail in Chapter 3. Names are usually allocated at the time of accessioning using the name that the plant was initially identified as (for collected plants) or sold or offered as by the nursery or donor. When cataloguing existing groups of trees and shrubs, mapping and numbering is often carried out prior to full identification.

TABLE 7. PLANT RECORDS.

		DESCRIPTION	PURPOSE
ALL PLANTS OF A TAXON	Author	This is linked to the botanical name. It shows which authority is being used; for example, *Acer campestre* L. shows that it is the name given by Linnaeus.	To ensure clarity. Some plants may be known by different botanical names, and it is important to know which one is being used to avoid ambiguity.
	Family	The plant family into which the plant is classified.	Useful for staff or visitors wanting to understand plant relationships. It can also be useful for producing lists of plants in a particular family. For inclusion on labels.
	Origin	The natural range of the taxon.	For staff and visitor interest and inclusion on labels.
	Habit	Evergreen, deciduous, climber, shrub, tree, etc.	For general information about the mix of the collection.
	Conservation status	Lists researched and published by International Union for the Conservation of Nature (IUCN). Plants categorised according to the level of threat to their survival.	To measure the value of the collection for plant conservation and for visitor interpretation purposes.
INDIVIDUAL PLANTS OR ACCESSIONS	Plant type	Original accessioned material—seed, cutting, plant, etc.	To help track plant's development.
	Propagation records	Often referred to as plant development records, these include information about techniques used, rates of success, and numbers of plants produced.	To monitor success of techniques used and numbers of plants being produced.
	Verification	Often a simple yes/no. If yes, who identified the plant and what sources of reference were used? Has it changed its name or been reidentified? If so, previous names should be recorded.	To indicate the level of confidence in the identification and provide reference in the future.

TABLE 7. PLANT RECORDS (continued).

		DESCRIPTION	PURPOSE
INDIVIDUAL PLANTS OR ACCESSIONS (continued)	Management records	Relevant information about the individual plant's mainte-nance. Major pruning, dam-age, pests and diseases, other notable work.	Many uses, including safety management, informing future maintenance practice, etc.
	Individual characteristics	Flower colour, flowering dates. This may be recorded photographically.	Many uses, including aid to identification.
	Dimensions	Usually height and girth or diameter. It is important to record the date measured to monitor growth.	To monitor rates of growth, ultimate size, and health. For unusual species it may provide reference data. It may also pro-vide visitor information for developing interpretation trails or lists of champion trees.
	Dead/alive	Is the plant alive or dead? If dead, why did it die?	To allow preparation of lists or maps of living plants only. Keeping records of dead plants is important for many reasons, including historical interest and as a back-reference from living offspring.
	Health	General or specific state of health.	To monitor disease or to prompt propagation.
	Provenance	May be described in detail and/or coded as follows: W = wild, G = garden, Z = from plant of wild provenance.	For general information or to judge the plant's possible value for conservation purposes.
	Sex	Male/female, for dioecious plants.	For possible propagation and study purposes.

In an ideal world, trees and shrubs brought into the collection would always be correctly identified and named, and there would be no need for any further attention. However, this is often not the case, and checking identifications and naming is an important management task, especially for scientific collections. There are two aspects to this checking or verification: firstly, that the plant is correctly identified, and secondly, that the name used is the preferred one under current nomenclature used for the collection. It should be remembered that plant taxonomy is not a static science, and names frequently change as our understanding of plant relationships develop. As well as incomplete naming, it is quite possible that names may change either through reidentification or revisions in taxonomic classification or naming. Plants obtained from commercial nurseries are particularly likely to come with out-of-date names, since companies are reluctant to change from those familiar to their customers. Both aspects of verification can be seen in the following example:

A tree has been accessioned with the name given by the donor—*Acer nikoense*, commonly known as Nikko maple. Verification by an expert in maples may conclude that the tree is misidentified and is actually *A. triflorum*, a related trifoliolate maple species. On the other hand, she may confirm the identification but rename the tree as *A. maximowiczianum*, the name adopted by the arboretum following a revision of nomenclature for maples.

Carrying on with this example, it is important to keep a record of previous names given to the plant, particularly where reidentification has occurred. It is also good practice to record the name of the person responsible for identifying a plant and what references were used. All this will allow people in the future to track and understand the level of authority and reliability of the identification. Many scientific collections use a numbering system to describe a plant's level of verification. The following levels are those recommended in *The Darwin Technical Manual for Botanic Gardens* (Leadlay and Greene 1998):

Level 0 Plant name not determined by any authority
Level 1 Plant name determined by comparison with other named
         plants

Level 2 Plant name determined by taxonomist using a library, herbarium, or other documented living plant material

Level 3 Plant name determined by taxonomist engaged in a revision of the family or genus

Level 4 Plant in question represents all or part of the type material on which the name was based or is a clone of it

Although verification using this or a similar system may be regarded as the ideal, for most collections it is more realistic to adopt a simpler yes/no system of verification with a name and any sources of reference used for identification and nomenclature. Table 9 shows how this information may be recorded.

All this may seem rather complicated and unnecessary for a simple local community or private collection, kept for personal pleasure or ornamental reasons. However, even here, it is good practice to question the identification of incoming plants and compare them with similarly named ones in other collections. After all, one of the pleasures of keeping a collection is the opportunity to study the plants closely to develop one's knowledge. Where doubt exists or confusion reigns, there are often local experts willing to give advice to fellow collectors and help with identification problems. Joining societies or networks such as the International Oak Society or the American Public Gardens Association is a good way for collectors to meet people with the knowledge to help.

Unidentified plants. Sometimes a plant may be accessioned that has not been identified, or only partially so. This is a common occurrence when plants are collected during expeditions. Provided other information relating to them is kept, even unidentified plants may become very valuable once identified and should not be discarded without consideration. Until full identification has been carried out, naming should be as complete as can be confidently achieved without guessing. It's much better to err on the side of caution; otherwise, it may be assumed later that the identification was based on thorough knowledge rather than a hunch! For example, a tree may be known to be an oak of some kind, but the species remains to be determined. For the time being its name will be simply *Quercus*, or perhaps *Quercus* sp. (the abbreviation for "species," to indicate the missing epithet).

Provenance or source. For a tree or shrub collected in the wild, the provenance is where it was naturally growing when collected. This is an important thing to record since species of plants show subtle variation from one part of their natural range to another, and gaining an understanding of this requires knowledge of the place of collection. For other cultivated plants, provenance could be the name of the nursery, collection, or garden; these are also often referred to as the source. It is important not to confuse provenance or source with origin, the latter referring to the natural range of the species or taxon in the wild. The origin will be constant for all members of the taxon in the collection, whereas the provenance is likely to vary from one accession to another. For example, *Quercus robur* (common oak, English oak) has a broad natural range through much of Europe, North Africa, and southwestern Asia, and this would be described as its origin. However, acorns may be accessioned following a collecting trip to a forest in Spain, and this location would be recorded as the provenance.

The level of precision required when recording provenance varies greatly depending on the information available and the intended use. For plants collected in the wild, precise locations (usually recorded as latitude and longitude) are important as well as altitude. Chapter 3 describes other information that may be recorded when plant collecting in the wild.

In the case of a seed or young tree sourced from another collection, it is useful to record the reference number used by the previous owner. This will make it possible to trace the plant's parent and obtain updates on information relating to it. This is particularly so for plants propagated asexually, where the propagules will be genetically identical to each other and the parent. For example, the parent plant may be of known wild origin, and the records relating to it will be valuable for judging the scientific or conservation value of its offspring. Likewise, surplus plants donated to other collectors should be supplied with their accession numbers and other relevant information. The details (contact addresses, etc.) of the recipients of these plants should also be recorded for future reference.

Location. Location within the arboretum may be shown very precisely with a dot or outline on a map, or less so as a grid reference or written description. This latter method is the one often used for herbaceous plants, where individual mapping is difficult to achieve and using bed numbers or something similar may be sufficient. But trees and shrubs tend to be large enough to be mapped individually, and this is the preferred option in most situations. As with all types of recording, it is useful to consider the use to which the maps will be put; keeping in mind who will use them will help you determine how precise they need to be. The subject of mapping is dealt with later in this chapter, under its own heading.

Measurement. Trees, and less often shrubs, are measured for a variety of reasons. It may be to provide a source of interest for visitors or valuable information about growth rates or ultimate sizes for horticultural reference. Where rare or unusual trees are being grown, the data may be of particular value since they may provide the only information on these species. Some collections make a theme of their largest trees and design trails with interpretation around them. Statistics, including measurements of size, can add to the interest of such trails. (PLATE 71)

Deciding whether or not to measure trees in a collection depends on available resources and the intended use of the information. It is often best to measure a selection or representative sample of trees at a frequency of, say, five years. Provided the date of measurement is recorded, the sequence of figures can provide a growth curve for each tree. This may become an interesting theme around which to develop a course of learning or a student project. By far the most commonly recorded dimensions are height and diameter. The latter must be measured at a set height above the ground (commonly 4 or 5 feet, 1.3 or 1.5m) in order to ensure consistency. Various measuring devices can be used, from tapes and mechanical clinometers to sophisticated digital instruments. Choice depends on level of precision, speed required, and budget. For occasional recording where speed is not a major consideration, normal tape measures can be used, though conversion from circumference to diameter will be necessary. For a small additional investment, foresters' diameter tapes allow direct reading of trunk diameter. (PLATE 72)

Plant health. Records of plant health may be kept for general or specific purposes. Monitoring the general well-being of the trees and shrubs is an important part of maintenance and can be done through regular formal inspections or by incidental observations by staff. As with other kinds of information, if recorded in a systematic and consistent way, health records can provide information about trends in diseases and may prompt and direct action to help avoid or remedy problems. Recording the reason for death or failure of plants can be particularly valuable for this purpose.

Health records, if made available to other bodies, may also contribute to the wider understanding or monitoring of particular pathogens, pests, or other agents. Some diseases and pests are sufficiently serious to require them to be reported to government agencies. Exotic insect pests imported via timber products are notable examples due to the risk they can pose to commercial and ornamental trees.

Arboricultural records

Alongside the records relating to the identification and sources of plants, most collections record information on their practical management. At the most basic level, recording planting and removal is an essential part of updating the list of living trees and shrubs growing in the arboretum. But recording the routine and occasional work carried out on individual trees and shrubs throughout their lives can serve many other purposes. The following are the most important.

Planning and monitoring maintenance work. Where maintenance is planned through work schedules, recording work completed plays an important part in monitoring progress. Information on the maintenance requirements of plants may also be recorded to aid work planning. For example, shrubs may be classified according to their pruning requirements or timing, allowing the production of lists of those needing attention in any particular month or season. These kinds of records may also help in preparing maintenance contracts with outside companies.

Management of tree safety. The primary reason for safety management of trees is to avoid damage and injuries resulting from falling limbs or other failures, but it must always be remembered that, should such an accident occur, records of inspection and any necessary remedial work may become legal evidence. It is therefore essential that these are kept in line with a written policy. In particular, dated records of inspection and completion of work must be kept and stored for a defined period of time.

Assessment of risk of tree failure is based on identifying features such as cracks, weak forks, and other faults. For this reason, safety records often identify and record these as a means of tracking changes in the condition of the tree and informing remedial work. For example, trees with braced limbs may be recorded in order that regular checks can be made on the cable tension or anchor points.

Monitoring management techniques. Trees and shrubs tend to be long-lived plants, and work carried out on them may have a significance for many years to come. Recording work may therefore help to judge the effectiveness of difference maintenance methods. For example, a range of different mulching materials may have been tried over the years for their effectiveness at suppressing weed competition. But unless records have been kept on which ones were used on which plants, along with some measure of success, it will be impossible to learn anything and adapt management accordingly.

Whether or not these practical management records are incorporated into the main plant database, or kept separately as management records, varies from one collection to another. Some collections utilise recording systems designed specifically for arboricultural purposes. These computerised packages combine mapping and recording facilities with predesigned forms for collecting standard information on the trees' physical characteristics and the management to be carried out on them. In many ways these systems are the arboricultural counterparts of computer systems for botanical records, such as BG-BASE, mentioned later in the chapter. They are designed primarily for managers of urban trees but transfer well to parkland and other situations. They place a strong emphasis on tree safety evaluation and standard arboricultural remedial techniques and may be less suitable for recording shrub maintenance and other more horticultural techniques. If using one of these packages, it is important that there is a reliable system of information transfer to and from the botanical records. In particular, additions and removals of plants must be communicated clearly to ensure both plant lists remain up to date.

Storage and retrieval of information

It is all very well collecting all the relevant information needed to adequately record and monitor a collection, but there's little point if it can't be easily accessed when needed. Traditionally, records were kept on paper or card indexes, but with the increasing availability, usability, and reduced cost of computers and software, these have become the standard tools for data storage. Not only do computer databases allow rapid retrieval of information, but they make it possible to produce selected lists for reference or dissemination of information to other collectors or interested parties. They also provide managers with a powerful tool for helping with the organisation and monitoring of practical work. For example, a database may be used to generate a list of trees requiring regular safety inspections or certain groups of shrubs needing regular pruning at a particular time of year. But to realise the full benefits of a modern computer database, it needs to be carefully constructed with data organised in a way that allows them to be sorted and filtered to extract the desired information for a particular need.

A database can be as simple as a spreadsheet with columns (or fields) for the various elements of information recorded. The first and most important of these are the accession number (with qualifier where needed or garden number where used), followed by the plant name and any other information considered relevant. Each line (or record) will therefore start with this unique number that can be used for relating the plant to a map location. Table 8 shows how a simple database might be organised. Note how the various elements of the plant names are split between different fields to allow easy filtering of information. For example, from this table it would be possible to extract a list showing all oaks or just a particular species, variety, or cultivar. This becomes much more difficult and time-consuming if the whole name is entered into one field. Likewise, other groups of data are given their own specific fields for the same reason. It is also good practice to enter data in a standard format for consistency and to avoid confusion. The second part of the accession number, for example, always contains four digits even for numbers below 1000. This table is sorted alphabetically by genus and then by species; where necessary, it could easily be changed to show sequence of planting or accession.

TABLE 8. SIMPLE DATABASE.

ACCESSION NUMBER	QUALIFIER	GENUS	SPECIES	VARIETY	CULTIVAR	PLANTED	SOURCE
2005/0675	A	Acer	distylum			2007	Hilliers
2005/0675	B	Acer	distylum			2007	Hilliers
2002/0043		Quercus	coccinea		Splendens	2005	Springfield Nurseries
2001/0024		Quercus	infectoria	veneris		2002	Global Trees
1989/0035		Rhododendron	arboreum		Album	1990	unknown

For simple collections where only basic information like that shown in Table 8 is being recorded, general-purpose office spreadsheet programs are quite sufficient. But for large amounts of complex information relating to many areas of interest or activity, specialised database programs may be needed to do the job. These not only give users a greater ability to perform complex searches (queries) and filtering of data but also allow the construction of a relational database, where a number of tables containing different kinds of information can be linked. For example, there may be extensive information about the verification of accessions including botanical notes written by those involved in checking identification and naming. It may be tempting just to create more fields in the existing table to hold all this information, but the danger is that the table will become too large and unwieldy, with data that is rarely used or only for specific purposes. It's better to create another table linked to the first by the accession number to hold all the information relating to these specific types of information. Table 9 shows how this may be done for the plants in Table 8.

TABLE 9. VERIFICATION TABLE.

ACCESSION NUMBER	VERIFICATION LEVEL	DATE VERIFIED	VERIFIER	REFERENCE SOURCE(S)
2005/0675	1	11/06/2006	JB Wood	Maples of the World
2002/0043	0			
2001/0024	1	08/05/2006	S Toomer	
1989/0035	1	19/04/2000	JB Wood	Herbarium ref: JL48/672

For large complex collections, plant databases can consist of many tables like this linked together by common fields. Of particular value for saving on data entry is a taxonomic table containing the information for each taxon in the collection. Botanical name, authority, origin, family, conservation status, and many other areas of information relate directly to the taxon rather than individual plants (see Table 7). By holding this information in a dedicated table with a code number for every taxon, each new accession can be allocated the correct code without the need for reentry of the name and all the other related information.

Off-the-shelf plant databases. To build a relational database like that described earlier from scratch requires a fairly high level of expertise, and for that reason many collections choose to purchase an off-the-shelf plant collection database. An example is BG-BASE, a software product used by many institutional botanic gardens and arboretums. The value of this kind of system is that the laborious work of building the database structure as well as producing lists of data to choose from has already been done. The most valuable of these data are the lists of plant names along with their associated authorities, plant families, origins, etc. The downside, though, is that these database packages are expensive to buy and limit the scope for individuals to customise their database for their own purpose. They also require a degree of training and database expertise to use. In the end, the choice comes down to individual need, budget available, expertise, and a range of other considerations. But as with most things, there's no point spending a lot of money buying a powerful tool like this and only using a small range of its functions.

Updating data. Plant collections by their nature are constantly changing. Trees are planted and removed; they grow, become ill, have limbs removed, or may even be reidentified. Information relating to the trees and shrubs must therefore be constantly updated to keep up with these changes and maintain the collection's value. In most collections, this role is given to an individual data manager or selected members of staff with the necessary training. Other members of staff requiring access to the data may be given a "read-only" version to access information. This is important to avoid misunderstanding, such as double entries, or corruption of data for other reasons. But responsibility for reporting changes lies with all members of garden staff. It is all too easy for tree removals or other work to go unreported unless a clear procedure of reporting is followed. Simple paper forms are a common way to do this, with entries for various kinds of information and dates for completion of work and database updating. With increasing use of handheld computers and wireless communication, there is the possibility of updating the database directly from anywhere in the garden as work is completed or necessary changes identified. Again, it is important to avoid the accidental corruption of the database from inputs like this, and it may be best to update temporary tables that can later be copied to the live database.

Data security. The data relating to a collection are enormously valuable and may be irretrievable if lost. It is therefore essential to establish a system of backing up to safeguard against computer crashes, office fires, or any other catastrophes. Regular copies of the data and maps may be made automatically or manually and kept in a separate location or remote computer memory. Whatever system is adopted, it should be regularly checked to ensure it is working.

Dissemination of records

The sharing of information with other collectors and interested individuals is an important function of many collections and one that is often written explicitly into their collection policies. As well as making available an up-to-date list of accessions, collections may share information relating to any research undertaken or techniques used to propagate and maintain plants. Increasingly this information is disseminated via Web sites, although some collections still produce regular reports and other written documents.

Conservation of many endangered species of plants, including trees and shrubs, requires cooperation between ex situ collections. Centralised databases of these rare plants growing in gardens are being developed to help in this. Of particular importance are the lists of "red listed" plants maintained by Botanic Gardens Conservation International (BGCI). Any collector can contribute their records to the list to help provide a comprehensive overview of the status of these species in cultivation.

Mapping

While databases provide a way of storing, arranging, and retrieving information about the trees and shrubs in a collection, maps show where they are and help link that information to the correct individual. This becomes particularly important when labels become detached, and location can provide a valuable means of identification. Maps allow quick location for staff and visitors alike and, as discussed in Chapter 4, provide a valuable tool for organising work schedules. As with databases, the level of sophistication required depends on the use to which they will be put. Simple hand-drawn maps may be perfectly sufficient, particularly where the purpose is just to differentiate between one tree and the next. The trees and shrubs may be shown as dots or other shapes, annotated with their accession or garden numbers. Where these maps are intended for use by visitors, more attention may be paid to visual appearance and other features and facilities. They may also be accompanied by a list of trees relating to the numbered dots to allow identification of the plants. Maps like this need a master version from which all others are copied. This master must be regularly updated as trees are planted or removed, or new paths or other features added. Tracing paper and pens are the traditional tools for mapping of this kind, and the resulting maps are often remarkably detailed representations of the arboretum. (PLATE 73)

Computer-based mapping

As with data storage, computers are increasingly taking over from paper maps, with software available at almost any level of sophistication. Not only do these have the benefit of quick and easy updating but, as with computer databases, they can be manipulated to show different ranges of information for different purposes. These so-called Geographic Information Systems (GIS) are used extensively for recording land use patterns in agriculture and forestry and are ideal for tree collections. By combining database and locational (geographical) information, these mapping systems allow a seamless and constantly updated relationship between maps and the information relating to them. The maps themselves comprise different layers or themes to show different area, line, or point features. For tree collectors, the most important theme is that of the trees and shrubs themselves. They can be plotted as points, or areas to represent their shape and size, and many systems provide a choice of symbols that can be used to differentiate between different plant types—conifers, broadleaves, shrubs, etc. Other features (roads, paths, grassland, buildings) can be added or removed like layers of electronic tracing paper to build up the desired map for a particular purpose. These maps can also be viewed at different scales and, since they are linked to the plant database, used to find a particular species or individual tree. (PLATE 74)

Surveying

Any kind of map is only as good as the accuracy of the surveying used to create it. Most maps begin with a background upon which the local features can be plotted. These background maps may be obtained from wider maps of the area in paper or electronic forms. The trees and shrubs themselves can then be plotted in their correct locations in relation to other features on the map. Surveying techniques using compass bearings and distances from other mapped objects is the traditional way to do this and remains a perfectly good approach in many situations. Positions measured by this method can then be plotted onto paper or GIS maps. Increasingly, Global Positioning System (GPS) technology is being used to map plant collections. Levels of accuracy and precision have improved greatly in recent years, and small handheld models designed mostly for outdoor leisure can be used quite successfully to map trees to an accuracy of a couple of metres or so. In addition, the coordinates generated can be transferred directly to GIS maps, so removing the need for replotting.

But GPS is not without its problems and shortcomings, and these should be clearly considered before the equipment is bought and used. Firstly, the levels of accuracy quoted by manufacturers tend to be the best possible in optimum conditions. The actual performance in practice is often much lower for various reasons. Of particular relevance in an arboretum is that accuracy is greatly reduced when working beneath a canopy of leaves—not uncommon in a mature collection or woodland. Since positions determined by this method use satellites for reference, good results also require that other features shown on the maps have been plotted accurately if they are to relate to each other. It may be useless to plot super-accurately surveyed trees onto a background map surveyed using less accurate methods. It would be better to save money and plot the trees by eye to match the existing features shown on the map. After all, the primary purpose of these maps is to differentiate the trees from one another, not determine their absolute position in relation to satellites! (PLATE 75)

Labelling

Labelling of plants at all stages in their life cycle is an important part of managing a tree collection. As plants pass through the propagation process from seed tray to pot and on to being planted out in the garden, a succession of labels should accompany them to ensure continuity of records. At the most basic level, labels are used by staff to show the plant's name and accession number and thereby provide a reliable link with the records relating to it. Without secure labelling, plants that may have cost large sums of money to collect, raise, and plant can become impossible to link with their records.

For most collections, labels fulfil more than the basic function of differentiating one accession from another. They are also one of the most important means of communicating information to visitors. These people may not have access to the extensive records relating to the tree concerned, and the label is likely to be their main source of information. Labelling is therefore the most basic form of interpretation relating to the tree collection.

Types of labels

As well as having to serve various functions for different kinds of users, labels need to come in many shapes, sizes, and degrees of permanence to suit the diversity of the plants to which they are attached.

Basic identification labels. Labels serving the basic function of showing accession number and perhaps name can be small, cheap, and simple to produce. They will usually be used by staff for the purely functional purposes of distinguishing different accessions and avoiding mix-ups. Labels used during the propagation process will usually be of this kind. They include sticky labels or tags for bags containing seeds or cuttings, and tab-style labels for pots or seed trays.

Secondary or backup labels on mature specimen trees may also be of this kind. They may be used in the initial stage of surveying existing trees being incorporated into a collection or for newly planted ones as a stopgap until more permanent ones are produced. For flexibility and speed, these labels may be produced as they are needed with handheld printers or engravers. These labels are often used as the primary means of linking plants to their records, and secure attachment is an important consideration. (PLATE 76)

General tree labels. For specimen trees and shrubs growing in the collection, labels need to be bigger than those used purely for identification purposes, typically a little larger than a credit card. Layout of text varies greatly but should be consistent within the collection, with clear type and a range of information to inform readers. In addition to botanical plant name and unique reference number, the most commonly included types of information are common name, family name, planting year, country of origin, and date of introduction.

The most common materials for labels of this kind are engraved plastic or stamped aluminium. Labels may be attached directly to trunks or branches, or located close to the plant on a post or stand. The most suitable method of attachment depends on local circumstances, and each has advantages and potential problems, as shown in Table 10. Although secure attachment is important to reduce waste and avoid disappointed visitors, labels such as these should not be relied on as the only way to link plants with their records. Accurate mapping and more robust secondary labels should provide a secure backup in case labels are lost. (PLATES 77–81)

The amount and type of information provided on these labels varies from one collection to another, but Plate 82 shows a typical tree label

TABLE 10. LABELLING METHODS.

ATTACHMENT POINT	ATTACHMENT METHOD	ADVANTAGES	DISADVANTAGES
Trunks	Screws and nails—plastic or metal. To allow for growth, fixings should be left proud, or springs may be inserted behind screw or nail.	Cheap. Labels can be positioned at eye level and usually remain unobscured.	Invasive—drilling trees is potentially damaging. Fast-growing trees may outgrow labels quickly. Metal fixings may be a problem for future sawyers!
Branches	Ties—plastic cable ties or wire.	Cheap. Non-invasive—no drilling. Labels can be positioned at eye level.	Labels easily obscured by leaves and may be shed with branches. Wire ties can cause damage unless regularly monitored.
Post or stake adjacent to plant	Screws or nails to post.	Non-invasive. Labels remain visible but may be too low for easy reading.	More expensive. Can get in the way of operations like grass cutting. May be time-consuming to make and erect.
Label stands and plinths adjacent to plant	As designed.	Non-invasive. Labels remain visible but may be too low for easy reading. Quick to erect.	Expensive. Can get in the way of operations like grass cutting.

showing a common layout. The design and choice of materials can vary greatly from simple engraved metal or plastic rectangles to more individual ones made of wood or cast iron. The latter kinds are more expensive to produce but may reflect the arboretum's "brand" and supports its individuality. For garden collections with a particular historical or design aesthetic, this may be reflected in the labels as well as other interpretation and signage. To support equality of access to information for blind visitors, all or some labels may be produced with Braille type.

It is important for ease of use that, whatever design is chosen, the layout of garden labels remain consistent for all plants in the collection. It is also important to resist the temptation to cram as much information onto a label as possible. Not only does this reduce the label's readability but may also increase its size to a point where it becomes visually intrusive. To convey more detailed information, it's better to use a well-designed plinth, though these have their own impact on landscape quality and can get in the way of grass cutting and other maintenance operations. Where these issues are a concern, leaflets with information covering a number of trees may be the answer, or even provision of visitor access to the collection database. These and other matters to do with interpretive media are covered in more detail in Chapter 6.

Obtaining labels—homemade or bought to order

As already mentioned, many collections use handheld label printers to produce backup labels or simple temporary labels for seed trays and plant pots; however, for garden labels, most collections, and particularly small ones, turn to external sources. Many companies produce labels for general use, and these may be fine for small numbers of simple labels. But when it comes to regular orders of labels showing a variety of plant information, it's usually best to use a company specialising in supplying botanical collections. Such companies have the benefits of being familiar with botanical naming and the information layouts commonly used. They will also be set up to receive information generated from the database, thereby reducing the need for laborious rewriting of plant names, families, origins, etc. (PLATE 83)

6 ▲ Talking about Trees
Interpretation and Partnerships

Almost all tree collections have a need or desire to engage with people outside the immediate sphere of the owner and managers. For many public or institutional arboretums, the need to raise income from admission charges or justify public expenditure makes it necessary to raise awareness of their work and promote use and appreciation of their resource. There are many mechanisms by which this communication can take place, from information boards and other physical installations through guided walks programs to Web sites and e-newsletters. In addition to explaining the work and role of the collection, it may be possible to use these channels of communication to extend learning and information beyond the boundaries of the arboretum to the significance of trees in the wider world. In large arboretums, these areas of work are sufficiently important to merit the employment of specific members or even groups of staff. Even in more modest ones, a relatively small investment in time or money can greatly increase the value of the collection for visitors. And as well as informing people, modern plant collections are increasingly keen to involve communities in their work to harness expertise and enthusiasm and meet a desire for inclusion and consultation. Participation in partnerships and networks with other arboretums and botanical collections to share expertise and cooperate in joint projects may also bring great advantages.

This chapter deals with many aspects of the ways collections can enhance their work through communication, partnerships, and public involvement and help ensure that they remain relevant and valued.

Interpretation

Almost all tree collectors, whether they are private individuals or public institutions, want to tell people about their collection. This may be as simple as offering the names of the trees and where they come from, but often the information communicated is much more detailed. Arboretums, like other kinds of collections, usually use the term "interpretation" to describe these means of communication. There are many definitions and ways of explaining what is meant by interpretation. Some people use the word in a rather literal sense to mean the mechanisms, such as information plinths and other media, created with the specific intention of imparting information. Others widen the meaning to include subconscious and spiritual influences—perhaps artistic interpretations—that may change someone's perception or feeling about something:

The following are three definitions that sum up what we usually mean by the term:

▲ "[Interpretation is] a communication process that delivers messages that connect with the interest of the audience and reveals meanings about a resource." (Brochu and Merriman 2007)
▲ "[Interpretation is] sharing your enthusiasm for somewhere or something that is significant." (Carter 1997)
▲ "Through interpretation, understanding; through understanding, appreciation; through appreciation, protection." (Tilden 1957)

The last of these indicates that, as well as a means of providing information, interpretation may be used to influence people's opinions and even their behaviour. (PLATE 84)

However you define it, interpretation has the potential to transform a tree collection from an attractive place in which to spend time and relax, into a valuable resource for learning and appreciation. The value of an anonymous pathside tree may be enhanced by the simple addition of a label to tell people what it is and where it comes from, but to realise its full potential may require an explanation of the medicinal qualities of its bark or use of its wood for making everyday items. (PLATE 85)

Like all other aspects of arboretum management, interpretation will have, at its source, the mission and overall objectives. If programs of interpretation are a major part of the collection's mission requiring substantial financial and physical resourcing, they will be recognised in the master plan. This may go as far as making provision for a visitor interpretation kiosk or a series of information boards or other installations, perhaps linked to thematic collections of trees and shrubs. (PLATES 86 AND 87)

Whatever the physical representation of interpretation, the important thing is that it supports a carefully considered strategy with clear objectives. Too often, interpretation is regarded as an add-on to the main business, thought about at the last minute when everything else has been done—and often too late! Rather, planning for interpretation should take place simultaneously with that of the collection itself and the physical aspects of the site. It may well be that the desire to communicate with visitors will influence the arrangement of the collection itself or even its species content.

Interpretation planning

In order to come up with a coherent interpretive plan, it is useful to first consider the sequence of interaction between the visitor and arboretum. In many cases, this begins before the visitor has even arrived at the entrance gate and may carry on long after they have left. Figure 3 represents the various phases of a visitor's experience defined by Lisa Brochu, a leading specialist in interpretive planning. Considering the collection from a visitor's perspective in this way can greatly help to order and arrange the various kinds of interpretation. A balance of different and appropriate kinds of interpretation (messages and media) can be planned to cover the various phases and provide visitors with the information they need.

The first or **decision phase** is when visitors may be encouraged to pay a visit by publicity material, a Web site, or press coverage. It may be

FIGURE 3. VISITOR EXPERIENCE MODEL
(Brochu 2003).

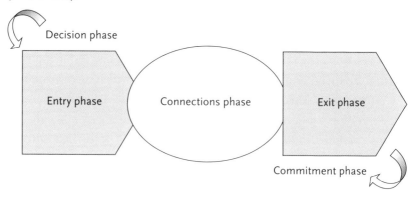

their first awareness that the collection even exists, and so interpretation in this phase is also a valuable means of publicity.

The **entry phase** is usually a visitor's first experience of the arboretum itself—at least on this visit. It should be where they experience a sense of arrival, are made to feel welcome, and begin to be influenced by the central interpretive messages. Guide leaflets and maps may be provided in dispensers or given to visitors by admissions staff. Information at this point may have an important influence on the success of the visit. Are there any special events or guided walks taking place that day? Is there a particular route to follow to make the most of the interpretation, or are some areas closed due to storm damage or tree felling work? (PLATE 88)

The **connections phase** usually forms the main part of a visitor's experience and is where a variety of interpretive media may be used to develop awareness and add to their enjoyment. This interpretation may be arranged in a planned sequence or spread more randomly to allow visitors to discover it in their own way.

The **exit phase** involves reinforcement and consideration of the visit. It could include a visit to a shop or restaurant where the merchandise may reinforce or remind visitors of an interpretive message. Postcards could be printed on recycled card or wrapped in paper bags from sustainably managed forests. Calendars with seasonal photographs of the arboretum will remind visitors of their visit and encourage a return trip.

Even after a visit, people may continue to be influenced by the experience. Their new awareness of the need to conserve trees and forests may influence their buying habits. Some visitors will become long-term supporters of the collection, and their continuing commitment may be nurtured with newsletters and other reminders. This may be described as the **commitment phase.**

Even with an appreciation of the visitor experience model, there are still many decisions to be made in drawing up an interpretation plan. A natural inclination for passionate tree collectors is to bypass some of the decision-making stages to get on to what they really want to express about their trees in an unstructured way. The first risk of doing it this way is misjudging the audience, with the result that many visitors may be confused or alienated right from the start. Another is the danger of creating something bland and uninspiring by automatically adopting means of interpretation that are familiar from visits to other sites or previous experience. More consideration and an open-minded approach may reveal ways to interpret in a more innovative or distinctive way. And as well as the visitors themselves, it is important to consider the practical and financial needs of the site and staff. What is the available budget for writing, construction, and maintenance? Are there landscape issues or health and safety considerations?

Before setting off on the potentially expensive road to the perfect interpretation solution, it is important to consider a range of questions.

Why provide interpretation?

The most obvious source of answers to this question comes from the collection's objectives. However, these overriding objectives cover various areas of activity and cannot provide sufficient detail within each. Objectives for interpretation must therefore be further developed and described. Although they will vary from one collection to another, in any arboretum the principal aim will almost certainly be to enthuse and inform people about trees, both within the collection and perhaps more generally. Staff within the arboretum will undoubtedly feel passionate about trees, and finding ways to communicate this will be an important part of interpretation delivery. Where collections are part of a wider organisation there may be an emphasis toward the objectives of that organisation whether it be environmental, cultural, or some other area of significance. A government-funded arboretum may emphasise current environmental issues such as sustainability or climate change, whereas a small community one may be more interested in local historical aspects.

In the first chapter we saw that many collections include in their mission or objectives at least one statement that relates to interpretation and learning. The mission of the National Arboretum of New Zealand at Eastwoodhill refers to this area directly: "To foster understanding and appreciation of nature by education, research and enjoyment of our unique plant collection." This gives plenty of scope for imagination and the challenge for staff will be to identify more specific areas of activity. One of the three objectives of the Waite Arboretum, Adelaide, Australia, is more specific: "To demonstrate and evaluate the suitability of a wide range of Australian and exotic trees to the local environment." This statement provides more direct guidance to those planning interpretation. (PLATE 89)

As well as the inspirational interpretation about trees themselves, there are more basic considerations. Interpretation can play an important part in the practical management of a site. At the most basic level, there are the purely functional needs of helping visitors to find their way around the grounds and avoid dangerous situations. But even this can be achieved in a number of ways and can, if done badly, jeopardise the relationship between the arboretum and its visitors. Blatant KEEP OFF THE GRASS! signs do nothing to engender a feeling of welcome, and better results can be achieved by more subtle methods. On the more positive side, interpretation can help to fulfil financial needs by increasing the likelihood of visitors making a return visit, becoming involved as volunteers, or contributing financially through membership or donations.

Who benefits from interpretation?

This is perhaps the most important question and the one often given inadequate consideration. Before deciding on the ways that the broad interpretation objectives will be met, consideration should be given to the people who visit the collection and the variety of needs and desires for information they bring. For example, in an urban park situation the most likely users may be family groups or casual walkers. These people are unlikely to come specifically to learn about trees and probably want information that is easy to understand and can be read quickly as they pass. On the other hand, a dedicated arboretum is likely to have a different range of users, perhaps including school groups, college students, or amateur tree enthusiasts. These people will have different knowledge starting points, and a range of information is likely to be required. They may even want to pursue further study around subjects introduced on site through other Web-based media.

Tailoring interpretation according to the users and their needs is all very well, but to do so one must know who the users are. This information may come from various sources but is often gained from objective visitor surveys. Once completed, these provide valuable information for many areas of planning as well as interpretation. The data collected should include profiles for age and physical ability as well as numbers and seasonal variations. Surveys may also be used to seek the opinion of visitors on the interpretation they would like and, ultimately, what is provided already. This information can be used to create a blend of interpretation to meet the needs of the various user groups, adapted to their particular abilities or perhaps language requirements. It may also be used to target interpretation on particular groups that the survey reveals to be poorly catered for or considered to be a priority for some reason. The subject of survey and evaluation is dealt with in more detail later in the chapter.

Judging the needs of visitors, even once the visitor profile is understood, may not be straightforward. Good horticulturists aren't necessarily experienced interpreters or teachers, and many collections without specialist staff are well advised to seek advice from those with more knowledge in this area. Establishing links with local schools or other educational establishments is a good way to do this and may provide benefits for both sides. Trained teachers may help with writing styles and appropriate language for particular age or ability groups, while arboretum staff can suggest ideas for projects to support environmental areas of the school curriculum. Of course, this model for support works in reverse where tree collections are being started in schools or other non-horticultural establishments. (PLATE 90)

What to interpret

From the overall objectives for interpretation, a number of subject areas can be decided upon. At this stage there is no need to go into too much detail; the actual interpretation programs and media used will be dealt with later. The subjects are likely to include general ones, relating to trees and the wider environment, and local ones to do with the arboretum, its location, and management. These may be derived from particular strengths, specialism, or significance of the collection, or its location. The following are typical subjects:

- ▲ the arboretum—what is it and what is its purpose?
- ▲ layout and features
- ▲ history and heritage
- ▲ current ownership and management
- ▲ tree biology—what makes a tree different from other kinds of plants?
- ▲ the importance of trees and shrubs to human life
- ▲ the threats to trees and the importance of conservation and sustainable use
- ▲ management of trees and shrubs—arboriculture and forestry

From subjects to themes. Each of these subject areas can be broken down further into more specific ones. For example, from the subject of tree biology, the difference between woody and herbaceous plants may be chosen. There is also plenty of opportunity to combine subjects: coverage of the purpose of the arboretum will almost certainly include the subjects of arboriculture and conservation. We are now getting to the level of individual interpretive messages, often known as themes, which are the intended messages that people will take away with them as a result of their visit. They should be clear and specific, and deciding what they are can help interpretation managers plan and run their programs in a logical and coherent way. Going back to the earlier example, from the subject of the distinction between trees and other plants, the following theme can be developed: "Trees have evolved a woody trunk and branch structure to grow tall and compete for light."

This concentration on one simple idea is an important function of determining themes. Trying to cover too many ideas at once is a common pitfall of interpretation and one that runs the risk of confusion and failure to deliver any of them. Indeed, it is a sign of success, not failure, if people go away from their visit having gained an insight into a subject but wanting to find out more. Short, single-sentence statements like the one just given usually make the best themes. Not only do they break down otherwise bewilderingly large subjects into more manageable chunks, they make it possible to judge the effectiveness of interpretive programs: at the end of their visit, do people know why trees are so large and how they get that way? Once determined, a theme can become the interpretive focal point for a trail, guided walk, or educational lesson, providing a thread to link apparently unrelated facts, trees, or places.

To increase the chance of engaging people's imagination, themes may be chosen that relate directly to their everyday lives. These kinds of themes may also serve the purpose of encouraging people to help conserve trees or forests by changing their patterns of consumption—for example: "We can all contribute to the conservation of natural forests by using wood products from certified sources."

How much and where? Cramming an arboretum with plinths, signs, and other physical means of interpretation not only detracts from its natural beauty but can make visitors feel intimidated and preached to. Gardens are, after all, places where people go to get away from the attention demands of modern life. It is therefore important to plan, not just the nature of the interpretation, its tone and design, but how much is appropriate and where it should be situated. The visitor experience model shown in Figure 3 demonstrates the need to consider the various phases of a visitor's interaction with the collection. Within the three central onsite phases, it is particularly important to think carefully about the impact of physical interpretation. Some garden managers consider almost any features to be unwanted intrusions that should be kept to a minimum. Others take a more relaxed approach and regard interpretive features as potentially attractive in themselves and an intrinsic part of the arboretum landscape. Neither side is wrong, and much depends on the atmosphere that is being sought; in an historical landscape without a precedent for signs and plinths, they are likely to look out of place, whereas they will be more appropriate in a modern garden with a more urban feel. The challenge is to find the right balance between providing information but avoiding possible intrusion.

Different arboretums deal with the challenge in different ways. Some put all but essential interpretation on leaflets and other non-intrusive media, while others concentrate signs and plinths in certain areas while excluding it from others. A zoning system may be devised with a map and accompanying text to describe the levels and types of media permitted in each. Entrance and exit areas (equating to phases) and main routes may be regarded as the most suitable areas and the least likely to be adversely affected. Quieter glades, rides, and particularly attractive views may be left clear to retain their natural landscape. These different interpretive zones may also be reflected in the kinds of interpretive messages used. General introductory and background information (including a site map) is likely to be positioned at entrances. More specific information relating to particular plants, locations, or horticultural management is better located within the collection itself, with individual trees as illustration. (PLATE 91)

How to interpret—choice of media

Many people automatically think of interpretation as information boards, signs, and other forms of written, onsite media. But there is a whole range of alternatives to these traditional communication means, and the development of the Internet has presented more exciting possibilities. Some collections may opt for one or two media for simplicity, while others will use a wide range to suit different locations, themes, or visitor phases.

Personal interpretation. It is often said that the most effective forms of interpretation are those where information passes directly between people without the need for written or other kinds of media. For a start, it has been shown that people tend to remember much more when information has been conveyed this way. But as well as its effectiveness, this kind of interpretation can help to personalise a visit to an arboretum. It certainly provides opportunities for those with a passion in the collection to express it directly to the people they want to enthuse or influence. It may also be used to give visitors an insight into the experiences of those actively involved in managing the trees or even have a go themselves.

▲ Guided walks. Guided walks are one of the most common ways used to enhance visitors' experience. They may be led by specialist interpreters or arboricultural staff, and in many arboretums, volunteers play an important role as leaders of guided walks. A variety of walks may be organised from general introductory to more specialist ones concentrating on particular subjects. Plant identification walks are a popular example of the latter. They may be part of a planned schedule with regular departure times from a central point, or one-off walks organised on request. Different ability groups may be catered for by having walks of different lengths or terrain demands. They may also be planned seasonally or to introduce visitors to a new collection or other feature. For small community projects, it may be important to organise regular walks to build support among local residents. They may be publicised in local newspapers or notice boards and timed to coincide with national tree events such as Arbor Day or National Tree Week. (PLATE 92)

Although one of the most valuable components of a guided walk is the personality of the guide, as with other kinds of interpretation it is important that the information they impart and the style with which they deliver it have been carefully considered. The subjects and themes identified earlier should again provide the basis for deciding what to say, and the language used should be sensitive to the audience so as not to patronise or confuse. Guides given the freedom to simply make up a walk to suit their own area of interest are likely to end up with a dwindling group of bored or confused followers! On the other hand, planning should not be so prescriptive that it stifles the individuality and enthusiasm of the guide. Walks are often planned to follow set routes with stops along the way at particular trees or other features. It is useful to produce guide notes to provide a framework within which guides can work. These notes will make clear what the theme of the walk is and how the various stops contribute to the understanding of it. These notes should also provide a structure to the walk including an introduction and a roundup.

▲ Talks and exhibitions. Taking the work of the arboretum to an audience beyond those visiting directly may be an important way to communicate with a new group of people and increase support. Giving talks and running exhibitions are two traditional and very effective ways to do this. Gardening societies, rotary clubs, and other local groups are often keen to fill their evening talks programs, and the investment in time and effort can bring rewards in the form of new volunteers or financial sponsors. Talks like this may be considered to be a kind of indoor guided walk with slides substituting for stops to illustrate the themes intended to be covered. They have the great advantage of being weatherproof and can bring spring, summer, or autumn to a cold winter's evening!

▲ Courses and workshops. A whole range of courses or workshops may be organised to allow people to learn more about trees and their uses. These may be tutored by members of staff or local experts and craftspeople. For some people, connection with trees comes from making something practical or beautiful with wood or creating a work of art from leaves or other natural materials. More horticultural types may enroll in courses in propagation or other practical techniques.

Signs, plinths, and waymarkers. In an ideal world, visitors would all be shown around by knowledgeable and enthusiastic guides, but this is rarely possible and other, non-personal means of interpretation are required. The style and careful positioning of signs and maps is important both for their effectiveness and their impact on the aesthetic quality of the arboretum. Choice of materials, colour, size, and design should all be considered in relation to their function while being in keeping with the landscape. A rustic wooden sign, for example, will look better in a woodland garden than a stainless steel one. Longevity and resistance to weather are particularly important considerations, and there is usually a trade-off between cost and performance in this respect. (PLATE 93)

The provision of direction signs should be based on real visitor needs and aim to guide people to all the main areas of the arboretum and important facilities. Junctions of paths and main entrances and exits are the most important places to give people confidence and encouragement. (PLATES 94 and 95)

Direction signs may also be used to guide people around set routes, perhaps along a self-guided trail with an accompanying leaflet. They are also a useful tool for guiding visitors around temporary obstructions or potentially dangerous work sites. In this case they are best backed up with additional information boards to explain the reason for diversion or exclusion. By doing this, potential sources of annoyance at being excluded from a favourite area may be turned into an interpretive opportunity to explain a necessary management operation.

Maps showing the overall layout of the arboretum are best positioned at entrances or central points. On sites where a large map may be considered intrusive or liable to vandalism, an alternative option is to provide a map leaflet instead.

The most common way to communicate with visitors is by panel or plinth. These stalwarts of interpretation have stood the test of time and still provide the basic means of information provision for most gardens and arboretums. As with other forms of physical interpretation, the choice of materials and design is fundamental to the success of this medium. They must catch the visitor's attention and hold it long enough to convey the theme intended. A catchy title that introduces a clear theme and invites further investigating is a good start. The number of words should be limited to no more than 200. The text may be split into two sections with the basic simple information in the first, developed for more studious readers in the second. The size of text may be varied to reinforce the distinction between the two—larger in the first, smaller in the second. The style of writing, language, use of illustrations, and other design elements are all essential considerations. (PLATE 96)

As well as permanent panels, temporary or mobile plinths may be used to provide topical information relating to current work, short-term features, or even the dramatic flowering of a particular tree or shrub.

Leaflets and guide books. Arboretums may provide their visitors with a variety of written material to enhance the value of their visit and take home with them to read more. A blend of permanent (or at least long-term) and temporary literature works well to cover both general and topical information. These kinds of publications may be given free to visitors on entry or sold in a shop or kiosk.

▲ General arboretum guides. General information may be covered in a garden guide. It should include basic visitor information on opening times and charges and may include a map. Guides of this kind are also useful for giving visitors background information about ownership, management, and the mission for the collection. They may be highly designed and full colour or simple photocopied or printed sheets. Even the former are generally single folded A4 or A3 sheets to allow cheap reproduction. Most arboretums provide every entering visitor with a free guide of this kind, whether handed out personally or distributed via leaflet dispensers. Larger arboretums with the resources to do so may reprint the leaflet seasonally in order to give more topical information or to publicise upcoming events. Even in less well-off establishments, it is likely that these leaflets will need to be revised and reprinted every year or so to keep up with changes in the arboretum. (PLATE 97)

▲ Trail guides. Trail guides are more specific than general guides, although some collections combine the two functions in one leaflet. Self-guided trails are a substitute for personal guided walks, and for many visitors they provide a valuable focus for their visit. Though they can never hope to provide the same personal feel as a human guide, they have the obvious benefits of being independent of the need for staff or volunteers and set timetables. At least, the guide leaflet needs to introduce the trail and provide a map. It may also give information relating to stops along the way, shown by stop markers. Trails may be permanent, seasonal, general, or themed. They may also be targeted at particular visitor groups:

children's trails with objects to find along the way are particularly popular. As with guided walks, different ability levels may be catered for by having a variety of different length trails. (PLATES 98 AND 99)

▲ Guide books. For visitors wanting to learn more about the arboretum and its plants, the guide book provides a step up from the general guide leaflet. More background and detailed information is likely to be covered with photographs and more text. Books of this kind are usually sold to more knowledge-hungry visitors via shops and may provide a valuable source of income in addition to their interpretive function.

Sculptures and other features. The atmosphere of an arboretum may be enhanced by sculptures or other artistic or ornamental features. These may or may not have a direct relevance to the trees or landscape, but they should at least be sympathetic to them and not divert interest from the plants. They may be permanent or introduced as a temporary exhibition in response to a business need to broaden the appeal of the arboretum. Done carefully, they can achieve this and help to introduce a new audience to the collection itself. (PLATE 100)

Children's play facilities. Play is one of the most effective means through which children learn. Tree- or forest-themed play facilities can serve the dual functions of both interpretation and a means of popularising the arboretum for children and their families. (PLATE 101)

Electronic, broadcast, and Web-based media. A number of modern forms of media have been developed to complement leaflets and other written means of interpretation. Video loops, often located in visitor centres, once formed the mainstay of these. Although video remains popular, particularly for the entry phase of a visit, more mobile or remote media provide a range of other options.

▲ Audio tours and information kiosks. One of the most popular of these media is audio tours, where visitors can listen to a recorded commentary as they follow a set route or self-determined tour with stops. Increasingly, podcasts are being used to allow visitors to download these tours from the Web onto personal MP3 players or even while on site via mobile phones. This eliminates the need to buy and hire-out expensive handheld players. As well as a spoken commentary, podcasts can include dramatic sound effects to enhance the visitor's experience, perhaps transporting them to a subtropical forest or roaring sawmill. (PLATE 102)

Some botanical gardens and arboretums have introduced interactive information kiosks with screens to provide a variety of information. These rely on an electricity source either from the mains supply or solar panels.

▲ Web sites. Web sites have rapidly become one of the most important ways for collections to communicate. They provide interpreters and those engaged in publicity with an enormous potential audience and a variety of communication possibilities. As well as conveying basic visitor information such as opening times and charges, they are invaluable for delivering interpretive themes in ways that may not be possible on site. They have the benefit of being easily and cheaply updatable and can reach and influence people who may never actually visit the collection itself due to geographical remoteness, disability, or some other reason. They play an important role in the decision and commitment phases of visitor experience described earlier in the chapter by engaging potential visitors on the one hand and providing a means of maintaining continued commitment on the other.

Traditional forms of communication such as newsletters and information packs can easily be transferred to Web pages along with more innovative ones such as interactive maps to provide virtual visitors with detailed information about the collection. Web sites may be linked to those of partner organisations for mutual benefit and cost saving on repetitive development of similar information.

▲ TV, radio, and newspapers. Local and national news agencies are always on the lookout for stories to feature, and occasional press coverage is a useful way for collections to raise or maintain awareness of their work. A particularly fine autumn colour display or the accession of a new and rare species of shrub may make a good story and have the side benefit of raising visitor numbers. Producers are often keen to interview those actually involved in the work being covered rather than PR specialists, and this is an opportunity for staff to express their enthusiasm and knowledge. Local radio or newspapers may welcome the offer to provide an expert for "Gardeners' Questions and Answers," and there will inevitably be opportunities to make reference to the collection and its work.

Interpretation centres and other specialist locations

Interpretation centres are the flagships of the world of information provision. They may contain a range of media—information boards and interactive displays, video loops and workshop sessions—all under one roof. These functions are often combined with other visitor services, such as a central information point or a place to join a Friends group. The value of these centralised interpretive facilities is their potential to become information hubs for the arboretum. Even visitors not naturally inclined to read plinths may be attracted to them for their promise of a different kind of experience. They also make possible forms of interpretation that would be impractical or inappropriate in outdoor or dispersed locations (hi-tech interactive installations, video displays, and slide shows, for example). But despite the benefits of these centres, they are by no means universally admired. Arboretums are, after all, outdoor places, and these centres are almost inevitably once-removed from the trees and shrubs themselves. They are also expensive to build and maintain and may actually have the effect of diverting people away from the main features of the arboretum—the trees. (PLATE 103)

Events and open days

Events may be organised purely as a means of raising money with very little connection to the collection itself. Although these kinds of events may provide income to support the management of the collection, they run the risk of diverting effort from the mission and losing the interest of staff and committed supporters. On the other hand, tree- or environment-related events may provide a focus for a range of interpretation and public involvement. They may be organised as regular fixtures in the calendar or as part of wider national events such as Arbor Day. Schools, community groups, or charities may be invited to take part. For budding collections, events like these can play an important role in their establishment by raising awareness of their presence and gaining support through publicity. (PLATE 104)

Arboretum staff members are often unaware of just how fascinating their work can be to visitors and the general public. Open days can provide a window on the arboricultural and other maintenance work of the collection and even allow people to have a go themselves. A program of guided walks, talks, and demonstrations can make for a great day out and may attract some visitors who would not normally pay a visit. With this in mind, these days may be advertised as special free-entry events aimed at widening awareness. (PLATE 105)

Did it work and how can we make it better?

Evaluation and review are as important for interpretation as they are in other areas of management. From a practical point of view it is important to know if the money and effort expended is meeting its objectives.

Testing, testing. For expensive interpretation such as permanent signs, plinths, and long-run literature, it is usually advisable to trial it in a temporary form before investing in the finished product. This may be done by producing laminated mock-ups of information plinths or draft copies of leaflets or audio recordings. The latter may be distributed to selected readers, but for fabricated signs and plinths there is no substitute for a real-life trial in the intended position. Only then can the text size, clarity, and relationship to the features being interpreted be properly judged.

Evaluation. If the intended interpretation has been developed with a clear theme, it should be relatively simple to judge success. Have readers/listeners gained the knowledge intended? Care should be taken, of course, since some people may already have been aware of what you are seeking to impart; remember that "added value" is what is being sought. In most situations the best way to discover this is by carrying out visitor questionnaire surveys. These may be randomised (every tenth visitor say) or targeted to particular groups of people for whom the interpretation was focussed. Sufficient numbers of completed questionnaires should be collected in order to get a valid measure of success, and it may be necessary to carry out the survey at different times and on different days of the week to capture various user groups. Questions must be carefully chosen and be consistently asked and recorded. As well as testing the success of delivering specific interpretive themes, questions may enquire about a respondent's opinion of existing interpretation or other things they would like to see included—new media or different themes, for example.

Feedback. There is no point in carrying out surveys of this kind unless the results are used to make improvements. Results should be analysed and, where necessary, changes made or new features introduced. However, care should be taken not to try to respond to every individual's desire. No interpretation will suit everyone, and it is important that the subjects and media remain true to the arboretum's objectives.

Partnerships

The value and effectiveness of almost any tree collection can be greatly enhanced by cooperation with other individuals or institutions. Irrespective of its size or level of complexity, there will be areas of expertise not possessed by the owner or managers, and sharing skills or experience through partnerships can help fill these knowledge gaps to the mutual benefit of all involved. Some of the collection's objectives may extend far beyond the boundaries of the arboretum, and only by cooperation with others can real progress be made. Other partnerships may provide more practical help from people who want to become directly involved by volunteering their time and effort.

The means by which cooperation is achieved are many and diverse and may be based on communities of interest (those sharing the same objectives and interests) or locality (geographical neighbours). These two communities, though often overlapping, provide different opportunities, from fundraising and practical support to cooperation in global plant conservation strategies.

Friends groups

In the early stages of their establishment, many tree collections develop a supportive group of "Friends." Even for long-established ones, it is never too late to enlist the help of the more dedicated and regular visitors by providing an organisational structure for their support. For small community tree collections, groups like this are likely to form naturally from the initial group of enthusiasts, whose idea it was in the first place. The group may also become the principal body for overseeing maintenance and development, managing contracts for grass cutting, arboricultural operations, and so on. Members of the group are likely to be unpaid tree lovers who carry out this role in their spare time. The maintenance work being managed may be carried out by volunteer work parties at weekends or by local contractors who have an interest in the project and may be willing to give a discount on their normal rate.

For larger institutional collections with a paid staff, Friends groups play a more supporting role, backing up regular staff where help is needed. As well as a means of practical help, groups like this provide a link with the local community and a channel for communication and consultation. They may develop roles in fundraising and lobbying and become the organisational structure for volunteering. As the group grows, it is likely to become increasingly self-sufficient, developing its own structure for governance with representatives on the management body for the arboretum.

Most Friends groups are membership organisations. In return for an annual subscription, members enjoy free entry to the arboretum, a newsletter or magazine, and possibly discounts for events or purchases. Away-days to other gardens or programs of evening lectures may be organised. Some Friends groups even form partnerships themselves with equivalent groups from other arboretums. Reciprocal arrangements may be agreed whereby members enjoy the benefit of free entry to each other's gardens.

As well as the income derived directly from membership subscriptions, Friends groups can be highly effective fundraising bodies. In some countries, their charitable status may have fiscal benefits for funds raised through legacies or donations. After fundraising, probably the most valuable contribution made by Friends groups is in volunteering. There is almost no limit to the range of jobs that volunteers can take on, and some Friends groups develop to a point where volunteers are almost indistinguishable from paid staff. In many cases, volunteers become the public face of the arboretum, giving advice and guidance to visitors and helping to explain decisions taken by paid members of staff. For this reason, it is vital that they are well trained and kept informed about new developments. This may be achieved through a volunteers' newsletter or regular training sessions between staff and volunteers. For example, a new guided walk is likely to require training of volunteer guides to explain the route and theme. Likewise, the reason for changing the opening hours will need to be carefully explained to volunteers assisting at the information point. (PLATE 106)

As the role of volunteers develops, some paid staff may become resentful or nervous, and it is important to clearly define the distinction between the two and communicate this to both groups.

The list of tasks commonly undertaken by volunteers in public gardens and arboretums is long and varied. Many of the common ones are as follows:

▲ information and admissions assistants
▲ plant label checking and replacement
▲ shrub pruning, propagation, and other horticultural assistance
▲ guided walk leaders
▲ visitor surveys
▲ help with data entry and other records management
▲ educational support—supervising school groups, etc.
▲ events support
▲ technical expertise

Local partnerships

As well as Friends groups there are many other possibilities for local partnerships. Local flora and fauna groups may be willing to carry out wildlife surveys in return for access to the arboretum for workshops or wildlife forays by their members. Their advice and the species lists derived from these surveys may be a valuable source of interpretive material. Local craftspeople may cooperate in running workshops and courses to demonstrate the uses and properties of wood, and colleges with horticultural departments are often keen to find work experience placements for their students. The range of possible partnerships of this kind is enormous and can help broaden awareness of the collection to a range of people beyond its normal interest groups.

Plant networks

In Chapter 3 the important role of plant swapping between collectors was described. International exchange of seed via index semina is a well-established scheme and one that contributes greatly to the development of many small and large collections. But the potential for collections to work together for mutual benefit and to forward their aims goes far beyond plant swapping and seed exchange. Most issues and problems faced by plant collections are common to others and networks can be a valuable means of sharing experience and knowledge. For small or newly established collections, networks may be a way to make links with longer-established ones for support and advice. They may also allow them to contribute (albeit in a small way) to wider conservation or environmental projects.

Networks are often informal in their nature, perhaps coming about almost by accident following contacts between individuals with mutual interests or problems. Contact may be maintained through irregular visits to other partners' gardens or requests for plants or advice. More structured plant collection networks may operate at a national or international level. Some have groups within them specialising in trees and shrubs, but in most cases trees are not differentiated from other plants.

A global network. The best known international plant network is Botanic Gardens Conservation International (BGCI), a charity with hundreds of members all over the world, mostly gardens and arboretums. Among its various conservation and educational projects, BGCI runs the Global Trees Campaign aimed at conserving species threatened with extinction. In recent years oaks and magnolias have been foci for attention. In each case, the conservation status of species within the genera has been assessed. The help of botanic gardens and arboretums has then been enlisted to gather data on threatened species grown in ex situ collections so that effort can be coordinated to grow absent or under-represented taxa more widely. Even small, private collections can contribute to this work by submitting their species lists and growing rare or threatened taxa for conservation.

BGCI also provides advice and training, including a range of publications. *The Darwin Technical Manual for Botanic Gardens* (Leadlay and Greene 1998) has become a core document, offering guidance on a broad range of subjects relating to the management of botanical collections.

National networks. Many countries have national networks for gardens and botanical collections. In the USA, the Centre for Plant Conservation is a network of over thirty gardens and institutions dedicated to conserving native plant species. The American Public Gardens Association (APGA) has a more general remit and wider geographical range with over 500 member institutions located in all fifty U.S. states as well as Canada. The association's objective is to strengthen public gardens by supporting and promoting their work in horticultural display, education, research, and plant conservation. One of the association's most important programs is the North American Plant Collections Consortium (NAPCC), a network of botanical gardens and arboretums working to coordinate a continent-wide approach to plant preservation, and to promote high standards of plant collections management. Participating institutions commit to holding and developing collections of documented living plants according to professional standards of collections management. They share information with other institutions to compare holdings and identify duplications and gaps.

In Britain and Ireland, PlantNetwork is a national network of botanic gardens, arboretums, and other documented plant collections. It publishes a regular newsletter for members and facilitates communication and training through a program of conferences and workshops. The latter are usually held in members' gardens and cover subjects as diverse as tree-planting techniques, interpretation, and plant record keeping. Plant Heritage (formerly the National Council for the Conservation of Plants and Gardens) has the objective of promoting conservation of cultivated plants including cultivars. Its main means of achieving this is through the National Plant Collection Scheme, in which individuals or organisations "undertake to document, develop and preserve a comprehensive collection of one group of plants in trust for the future." Even very modest collections may contribute by developing specialist collections of less popular or uncommon genera.

Specialist interest groups. A number of specialist groups operate at both international and national levels. As well as being a great way to meet and exchange information with like-minded tree folk, they have a practical purpose in spurring cooperation on specific projects, such as seed-collecting trips. Some groups focus on particular genera; oaks, maples, and magnolias all have their own societies with a membership made up of individuals and gardens. The British Conifer Society and International Dendrology Society focus on a broader range of trees. All these organisations publish magazines or newsletters and hold occasional conferences and even international trips to places of tree-interest for their members. Some operate members' seed donation schemes. Web contacts for these and other organisations are listed on the next page.

Links to Tree Organisations and Networks

American Public Gardens Association (APGA)
www.publicgardens.org

Arboricultural Association
www.trees.org.uk

Botanic Gardens Conservation International (BGCI)
www.bgci.org

British Conifer Society
www.britishconifersociety.org.uk

International Dendrology Society
www.dendrology.org

International Oak Society
www.internationaloaksociety.org

International Society of Arboriculture (ISA)
www.isa-arbor.com

Magnolia Society International
www.magnoliasociety.org

Maple Society
www.maplesociety.org

Plant Heritage / National Council for the Conservation of Plants and
    Gardens (NCCPG)
www.nccpg.com

PlantNetwork
www.plantnetwork.org

Royal Horticultural Society
www.rhs.org.uk

RHS Plant Finder
www.rhs.org.uk/rhsplantfinder/plantfinder.asp

References and Further Reading

Brochu, Lisa. 2003. *Interpretive Planning: The 5-M Model for Successful Planning Projects*. InterpPress.

Brochu, Lisa, and Tim Merriman. 2007. *Personal Interpretation: Connecting Your Audience to Heritage Resources*. InterpPress.

Brown, George E. 2004. *The Pruning of Trees, Shrubs and Conifers*. 2nd ed., revised and enlarged by Tony Kirkham. Timber Press.

Buffin, Mike. 2007. *The Gardener's Guide to Planting and Growing Trees*. Lorenz Books.

Carter, James, ed. 1997. *A Sense of Place: An Interpretive Planning Handbook*. Tourism and Environment Initiative, Inverness.

Dirr, Michael A. 1997. *Dirr's Hardy Trees and Shrubs*. Timber Press.

Dirr, Michael A., and Charles W. Heuser, Jr. 2009. *The Reference Manual of Woody Plant Propagation*. 2nd ed. Timber Press.

Hillier, John, and Allen Coombes, eds. 2002. *The Hillier Manual of Trees and Shrubs*. David and Charles.

Leadlay, Etelka, and Jane Greene, eds. 1998. *The Darwin Technical Manual for Botanic Gardens*. Botanic Gardens Conservation International.

Lonsdale, David, ed. 1999. *The Principles of Tree Hazard Assessment and Management*. The Stationery Office.

Prendergast, Daniel, and Erin Prendergast. 2003. *The Tree Doctor: A Guide to Tree Care and Maintenance*. Firefly Books.

Shigo, Alex L. 1991. *Modern Arboriculture: A Systems Approach to the Care of Trees and Their Associates*. Shigo and Trees Associates.

Stearn, William T. 2002. *Stearn's Dictionary of Plant Names for Gardeners*. Timber Press.

Strouts, R. G., and T. G. Winter. 1994. *Diagnosis of Ill-Health in Trees.* The Stationery Office.

Thomas, Peter. 2000. *Trees: Their Natural History.* Cambridge University Press.

Tilden, Freeman. 1957. *Interpreting Our Heritage.* 3rd ed., 1977, University of North Carolina Press.

Toomer, Simon. 2005. *Trees for the Small Garden.* Timber Press.

Tudge, Colin. 2008. *The Tree: A Natural History of What Trees Are, How They Live, and Why They Matter.* Paw Prints.

Vertrees, J. D., and Peter Gregory. 2009. *Japanese Maples: The Complete Guide to Selection and Cultivation.* 4th ed. Timber Press.

Watkins, John, and Thomas Wright. 2007. *The Management and Maintenance of Historic Parks, Gardens and Landscapes.* Frances Lincoln.

Index